FRAME
Your Memories

FRAME
Your Memories

40 Simple Craft Projects to Personalize Your Family Treasures

Susie Johns

Reader's
Digest

The Reader's Digest Association, Inc.
Pleasantville, New York/Montreal/Sydney

A READER'S DIGEST BOOK

This edition published by The Reader's Digest Association, Inc.,
by arrangement with New Holland Publishers (UK) Ltd.

Garfield House, 86–88 Edgware Road
London W2 2EA
United Kingdom
www.newhollandpublishers.com

Projects on front cover: Left to right: Notes to Remember (page 88), Ribbon and Lace (page 130).

Projects on back cover: Top to bottom: Trinkets and Treasures (page 56), Tiled Treasures (page 106), Traveler's Tale (page 68), Memory Board (page 148), Candy and Glitter (page 98).

Projects on contents page: Left to right: A Clear Case (page 116), Trinkets and Treasures (page 56), Childhood Treasures (page 38).

FOR NEW HOLLAND
Senior Editor: Corinne Masciocchi
Design: Casebourne Rose Design
Photography: Shona Wood
Production: Hema Gohil
Editorial Direction: Rosemary Wilkinson

FOR READER'S DIGEST
U.S. Project Editor: Jane Townswick
Canadian Project Editor: Pamela Johnson
Copy Editor: Barbara Booth
Project Designer: Mabel Zorzano
Associate Art Director: George McKeon
Executive Editor, Trade Publishing: Dolores York
Associate Publisher, Trade Publishing: Rosanne McManus
President and Publisher, Trade Publishing: Harold Clarke

Library of Congress Cataloging in Publication Data:
Johns, Susie.
  Frame your memories : 40 simple craft projects to personalize your family treasures / Susie Johns.
    p. cm.
  Includes bibliographical references and index.
  ISBN 978-0-7621-0861-9
  1. Picture frames and framing. I. Title.
  TT899.2.J65 2007
  749'.7--dc22
                                                        2007013353

We are committed to both the quality of our products and the service we provide to our customers.
We value your comments, so please feel free to contact us.

    The Reader's Digest Association, Inc.
    Adult Trade Publishing
    Reader's Digest Road
    Pleasantville, NY 10570-7000

For more Reader's Digest products and information, visit our website:
        www.rd.com (in the United States)
        www.readersdigest.ca (in Canada)]
        www.readersdigest.com.au (in Australia)
        www.readersdigest.com.nz (in New Zealand)

NOTE TO OUR READERS

Reproduction by Pica Digital PTE Ltd, Singapore
Printing and binding by Times Offset, Malaysia

1 3 5 7 9 10 8 6 4 2

Contents

Introduction

Memories are unique and personal to each and every one of us. You may have a set of holiday photographs or sepia prints of your ancestors; you may cherish a special souvenir picture of a family wedding or anniversary or a portrait of a grandchild; you may have a valued watercolor painting bought on vacation or painted by a friend; or perhaps you have discovered an old map of a place in which you once lived, or a sketch of a faraway place you once visited.

While some personal souvenirs are best kept hidden away—love letters hidden among folds of silk in a dresser drawer, romantic photographs under lock and key in a special box, a fragile scrap of lace pressed between the pages of a favorite poetry book—there are other treasures that deserve to be put on display, such as a baby's footprint, a child's drawing, photographs of family and friends or of distant places and memorable events. What better way to show them off than in a customized frame, box, or album?

In *Frame Your Memories* you will find dozens of ideas for customizing frames to match or complement the picture or object inside. If you have more than one picture or object—in other words, too much to include in one frame—there are also ideas for boxes and albums that you will want to showcase.

Most of these projects require no special skills or equipment. Many of the techniques will be familiar to anyone who enjoys putting together scrapbooks or making cards or for those who sew a little or who are familiar with a paintbrush or a hammer and nails to tackle the occasional do-it-yourself job around the house.

And there's no need to spend a lot. Although the finished results, if you follow the step-by-step instructions with care, are impressive, many of the materials used are inexpensive. For example, the Fabulous Fresco frame on pages 34–37 requires only string and cardboard to create a finish reminiscent of old plaster, and the project on pages 116–119 recycles unwanted CD covers.

Before you embark on your chosen project or projects, make copies of your precious pictures or documents. These days it has never been easier to copy old photographs. Your local office-supply store, photo print store, or drugstore usually offer this service. Many printers attached to home computers also feature a copy function, and in this case it is simply a matter of buying good-quality printing paper to achieve satisfactory results. By making a photocopy, you will avoid the risk of damaging the original, and you may even want to make several copies to share with family or friends.

Look out for specialty printing papers, too. Try experimenting with textured types, like watercolor paper or canvas, and others that can be used to transfer pictures onto fabric and other surfaces.

Moreover, you can use the projects in this book as starting points for your own creativity. For example, the techniques for transferring photographs onto the lid of a box (see pages 137–140) could also be used for decorating an item of clothing; the découpage techniques used on the map frame (see pages 68–71) and the graduation frame (see pages 72–74) could be adapted to boxes, album covers, and even pieces of furniture. These techniques are so easy and straightforward that you'll be limited only by your imagination. Be creative—and enjoy framing your memories.

Susie Johns

  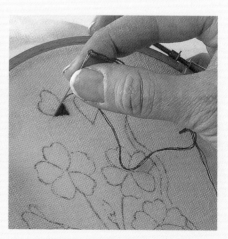

MATERIALS, TOOLS, AND
Techniques

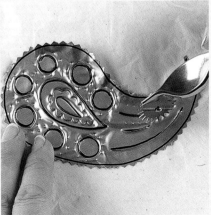

Materials and Tools

These days craft supplies can be found almost anywhere—from large craft-supply chains and specialty stores to mail-order catalogs and the Internet. But it is also fun to apply a little ingenuity. There are many items right in your own home that can be used for your projects, such as string, cartons, used postage stamps, and even broken or unwanted toys. Thrift stores, flea markets, and garage sales are also great sources of finds. Below is a list of useful materials and tools that were used to create the frames in this book, along with an explanation for reference. However, you may not need all of these; each individual project lists all of the materials and equipment necessary to make a stunning one-of-a-kind design to display your memories.

Paper, card, and metal leaf

For projects intended to last several lifetimes, many people prefer to use acid-free paper products: The choice is yours. Store materials flat in a box, file, or drawer, and be sure to save any small pieces left over from other projects. You never know when they may come in handy.

Card stock

This card is used by picture framers to create a border around pictures and to create a space between the surface of a picture and the glass. Thick and sturdy, it is available in a range of colors and finishes. To cut it, you will need a steel ruler and a sharp blade, not scissors.

Gray board

Cheaper than mat board and just as sturdy, gray board is useful for mats that are to be covered with decorative papers or other treatments and for constructing album covers. Gray board is often made from recycled paper.

Colored papers

These days you have plenty to choose from. Suppliers feature so many beautiful colored papers for letter writing, scrapbooking, and other crafts.

Printed papers

Stores selling scrapbooking and cardmaking supplies offer a range of printed papers for use as backgrounds.

Photocopies

Most of us have access to a photocopier, which is an invaluable tool not only for producing copies of

MATERIALS, TOOLS, AND TECHNIQUES

precious photographs (experiment with different types of photo-quality printing papers) but also for producing background papers by copying letters, postcards, or fabrics. For the Mini Album (pages 93–95) the floral paper used on the cover is a photocopy of a pretty cotton fabric. If you are pasting photocopies, try out a small piece first: Unlike laser copies, those made on inkjet machines sometimes dissolve when water-based glues are applied.

Gift wrap

Here is another product that will overwhelm you with the choices available. For craft projects try to use the best-quality gift wrap because the paper will be stronger and less prone to creasing.

Old letters

Beautiful handwriting on letters, cards, and envelopes can be very decorative and will add a personal touch to many projects. As you will no doubt wish to keep the originals, it is advisable to make photocopies.

Metal foil

Thin sheets of metal foil are an ideal material for covering frames and creating interesting effects. Available in various finishes, such as silver, gold, and bronze, thin sheet metal has been used on several of the projects in this book, such as Love Letters (pages 124–127), Lasting Impressions (pages 120–123), and Notes to Remember (pages 88–92). See page 23 for tips on how to emboss sheet metal.

Metal leaf

Gold leaf, made from thin sheets of real gold, has been used for centuries to gild furniture, walls, and picture frames. These days you can buy sheets of leaf metal, singly or in packets, in faux gold, silver, and other metallic effects, and it will not cost you a king's ransom. Very thin and fragile, this can be applied to surfaces for a rich metallic sheen and was used in the project A Glass Act (pages 60–62).

Brushes, paints, and varnishes

It is important to have the right brush for the job. Look after your brushes: A good brush, well cared for, will last a lifetime. Acrylic paints and varnishes are particularly tough on brushes unless you wash them out with plain or soapy water immediately after use. For artists brushes and paints in tubes and pots, check out your nearest art-supply store. It's also worth checking any local hardware stores for paints that are intended for walls and woodwork but which can also be used for crafts.

Pens and pencils

Permanent marker pens are useful for marking designs on various surfaces, including acetate, or when making stencils. An ordinary pencil is best for tracing and for lines that need to be erased later.

Artists brushes

When buying brushes, seek the advice of an expert. Any good art supplier will tell you which brush to use for any particular paint. As a rough guide, sable and squirrel-hair brushes—while perfect for watercolors because they hold a lot of paint and come to a fine point for painting small details—may be ruined if used for crafts. Most of the paints used in this book are acrylics, so synthetic brushes are probably the best bet, and you will find a good selection in most stores. Small round brushes are ideal for line and detail, and larger ones are best for painting bigger areas. Flats and filberts are used for broad strokes and backgrounds, and rigger brushes, with their long fine hairs, are excellent for painting thin lines.

Household brushes

Great for base coats and covering large areas, buy these at your local hardware store, but beware of "bargain" brushes; many cheaper types tend to shed their bristles.

Stencil brushes

These feature stiff bristles chopped off to produce a flat surface for dabbing on paint, and they are available in several sizes. Unless you plan to do a lot of stenciling, you could buy an inexpensive foam brush or simply use a small piece of synthetic sponge rather than investing in a special stencil brush.

Acrylic paints

Acrylic paints were developed early in the 20th century for mural painters and became widely available to artists in the 1950s. Ideal for crafts because they offer good coverage and a hardwearing surface, they are available in a wide range of intermixable colors. Most of the projects in this book use artists-quality acrylics in the softer-textured "flow" formula, available in tubes or tubs, rather than the more buttery-textured traditional acrylics. Acrylic paints are also sold under the label of deco paints, usually in a range of ready-mixed colors designed to appeal to crafters and home decorators. These are mainly found in small pots with a more liquid texture.

Latex household paint

Also known as emulsion paint, this is the usual choice for painting interior walls but can also be a good, economic choice for crafters. Plain white matte latex paint makes a good base for the application of acrylics, and colored latex paints are the perfect choice for certain paint effects, such as those used in Aged Beauty (pages 45–47).

Blackboard paint

As the name implies, this creates a surface like a traditional chalkboard and was used to great effect in School Spirit (pages 63–65). Most brands, which you will find in well-stocked hardware stores, are solvent-based and should be painted over a coat or two of universal primer. You will need to clean brushes in white spirit (or according to the instructions on the tin). If you shop carefully, you may be able to find a water-based version, but the surface may not be as durable or long-lasting.

Primer

Hardware stores sell universal primer and specialty primers for wood or metal, depending on the surface to be decorated. In this book most of the surfaces are wooden frames, so acrylic gesso primer, sold in art-supply stores, has been used as a base coat for all the

paint applications. Perhaps the most important consideration when painting the frame, before priming, is to make sure the surface is smooth and free from dust and grease so that any applications of paint will adhere to the surface and not peel or flake off as time goes by.

Paint pens

Essentially liquid poster paint in a pen with a felt nib, these are excellent for adding fine detail to painted surfaces—and can also be used on metal, glass, wood, rubber, and other surfaces.

Crackle varnish

Not to be confused with crackle glaze, which is a paint effect, this two-part varnish is usually used on top of decorative papers to give an effect like aged, slightly discolored varnish, with a network of tiny cracks. Paint is usually worked into the cracks to enhance them and make them more visible. The frame with a musical theme, Notes to Remember (pages 88–92), makes use of this treatment.

Accessories

To ensure good results, make sure you have sandpaper in fine and medium grade for preparing surfaces to be painted, along with plenty of rags or paper towels to wipe away spills.

CRACKLE GLAZE

For a cracked paint effect, such as that you would find on an old barn door, you need to apply a layer of paint, a layer of special crackle glaze, then another layer of paint on top; the glaze causes cracks to form in the top layer of paint. There are a number of products available in the shops, and results vary.

Cutting tools

Most of the projects in this book require some cutting, so you will need the right tool for the job.

Scissors

Large scissors will be needed for cutting sheets of paper and card stock, and small scissors with pointed blades for cutting out intricate shapes for decoupage. Have a good pair of dressmaker's shears for cutting fabric and do not be tempted to use these for card or paper. In craft shops you will also find a range of scissors with shaped cutting blades that are useful for making fancy paper borders.

Craft knife

Choose a good-quality knife with a replaceable blade—and make sure you replace the blade frequently; a dull blade is not as safe as a sharp one. The knife used to make the projects in this book is a scalpel with a size 10 blade, which has a long, sharp, angled edge for

cutting straight lines and a good point for cutting curves and stencil shapes.

Cutting mat

A self-healing rubber mat is essential when using a craft knife. An 11 x 17-inch size is good for most purposes, but if you tend to make only small-scale projects, you may find that an 8½ x 11-inch mat is adequate.

Steel ruler

A metal ruler, sometimes referred to as a straightedge, is essential for cutting straight lines when using a craft knife. A 12-inch ruler is adequate for most purposes.

Paper trimmer

If you are likely to be trimming a lot of photographs, you will find this to be a valuable tool.

Adhesives

It is important to choose the right adhesive, because the wrong type might ruin the finished result. It is best to use one that is solvent-free.

Household glue

Sometimes referred to as school glue or white glue, it is strong enough to adhere most items and a good choice for children. White in color and thick in texture, it dries clear. You can use it for a range of materials, including wood, card, and paper, but take care with very thin papers because it may cause wrinkling. Often the wrinkles disappear as the glue dries, but be sure to test a piece first before embarking on a big project.

Craft seal

Otherwise known as decoupage medium, this glue is similar to household glue but a thinner consistency and ideal for decoupage projects, both for sticking down paper pieces and brushing over the surface to produce a protective layer.

Craft adhesives

Play it safe and choose a glue specially formulated for certain materials, such as wood, metal foils, foam rubber, fabrics, mosaic tiles, and so on. Craft-supply stores offer a range of brands, so be sure to read the labels carefully.

All-purpose glue

This type of glue dispenses with the need to have different glues for different jobs—but do check the label for advice before using any product. Many all-purpose glues are solvent-based and therefore not suitable for use by small children.

Glue spreader

This plastic spreader with flexible tip is a useful tool and very inexpensive, though it is easy enough to improvise with a scrap of thick card or a piece cut from an old credit card. Think twice before plunging a good paintbrush into glue, because it may have to be thrown away afterward.

Printing, stamping, and stenciling

The techniques covered in this book are not too specialized, so even if you are tackling something you have not tried before, the chances are you will be familiar with the materials required.

Acetate

A thin, flexible, and transparent material perfect for creating stencils. Simply cut out the areas of design using a craft knife.

Tracing paper

Useful for tracing patterns from the back of the book, though you may prefer to use a photocopier.

Craft foam

Flexible sheets of colored foam to use in all sorts of ways. Here craft foam was used to create shapes to decorate frames (see Pet Friendly, pages 42–44) and also to make homemade rubber stamps (see page 24).

Ink stamp pad

These are available from most craft stores in a range of colors and are used for inking rubber stamps.

Fabrics

Fabrics can be a good choice for covering frames, and you have a wide range of colors, textures, and patterns to choose from. In most cases it is a good idea to apply a layer of batting to the front of the frame before stretching your chosen fabric over and securing it at the back. Use your fabric as is, or embellish it by sewing on buttons or beads (see examples on pages 130–133 and 137–140), or by embroidering (see Country Charm, pages 141–143).

Mosaic tiles and grout

One of the frames in the book features small glass tiles. These are sold in most craft stores. You can use household glue or a proprietary tile adhesive to fix the tiles to the frame. You will also need grout to fill in the spaces between the tiles. Grout is available in powder form to be mixed with water, or it can be purchased premixed and ready to use.

Beads, buttons, and shells

Buttons and beads add decorative detail, and most are inexpensive to buy. Depending on the covering of your frame or album, you can stitch or stick them in place. Shells can also be very decorative (see Ocean's Edge, pages 113–115). If you are buying shells, check that they have been gathered from a sustainable source.

Wooden shapes

Die-cut shapes from plywood, MDF, or balsa wood can be found in craft stores or cut yourself using a jigsaw. Smooth off rough edges with fine sandpaper before priming and painting.

Ribbons and braid

Ribbons, braid, and lace edgings add a pretty touch to craft projects, and there are so many widths, colors, and types available. Keep an eye out for wired-edge ribbons, which are great for making bows, and for self-adhesive ribbons, which can be used to create attractive borders.

Stickers

Check out the scrapbooking and cardmaking sections of a craft store or stationers for a dazzling array of stickers. They are a quick and easy way to add decorative detail.

Techniques

The projects in this book require no special skills or equipment. Many of the techniques will be familiar to anyone who enjoys scrapbooking or cardmaking, sews a little, or is familiar enough with a paintbrush or hammer and nails to tackle the occasional do-it-yourself job around the house. Each project has detailed step-by-step instructions and a list of materials needed, and, where space allows, additional ideas to inspire you. It is not necessary to follow the directions exactly, because your frame and picture may be bigger or smaller than the one used in the book. In this case, use the step-by-step instructions as a guideline only, adapting the measurements and quantities as required. The same applies to colors and patterns: You may wish to match a particular color scheme or suit your own individual tastes, so feel free to experiment and adapt.

Frame types

There are many different types of picture frames, and you will no doubt be dazzled by the sizes, shapes, and materials available. The different shapes include the swept frame, which has a high outside edge sweeping down in a curve to the sight edge (the edge surrounding the picture in the middle) and the reverse profile, with the thickest part of the frame nearest to the picture. For most of the frame projects in this book, however, these two types have not been used because a plain, flat frame has more potential when it comes to decorating.

You will, however, see as you turn the pages that a variety of shapes, sizes, and styles have been used and that the techniques can be adapted to what is available in your local store or what you have tucked away at home. It is important to note that while craft and

hobby stores and specialty framers have a wide array of ready-made frames to offer, you should extend your search to flea markets, thrift stores, charity stores, and garage sales because you may pick up a real bargain.

Do not ignore frames that are scratched, chipped, or tarnished, because even damaged frames can be given a new lease on life with clever decorative treatments. Many of the projects are well suited to reviving a damaged frame. The same applies to a frame that has been painted or varnished in an unattractive color, because you will probably be able to rub off the worst with sandpaper before repainting or recovering it.

Most frames consist of the same component parts: The frame itself, glass or acrylic, a mat, and a backing board. In most circumstances your picture will fit in between the mat and the backing board (though, as you will see, some of the projects defy these simple rules).

Before decorating a frame, you will need to deconstruct it. Many modern frames have removable clips holding the backing board in place; these are easy to remove and replace later. Others will be held in place with panel pins or small flat metal points that when removed, may have to be discarded and replaced with new ones from the hardware store.

If you have trouble replacing the backing board, you may need to seek the help of a professional picture framer.

Preparing a frame for decoration

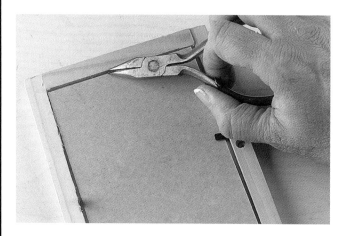

1 Many inexpensive frames have flat metal pins holding the backing board in place. In most cases these can be carefully bent back using small pliers.

2 Once the backing board and glass have been removed, you may need to sand a wooden frame before painting it or sticking anything on. Sanding removes old varnish or paint, smoothes rough edges, and helps new paint, varnish, or glue adhere to the surface.

3 A coat of primer protects the wood and provides a good base for painting or other decorative finishes. Acrylic gesso is a good primer for most paint finishes; household mat emulsion is a cheaper alternative. One or two coats may be necessary. Always let each coat dry before applying the next.

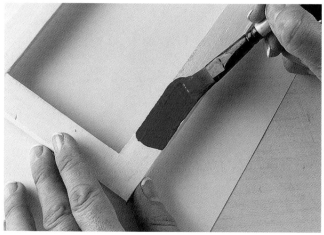

4 After one or two coats of primer, the frame is ready to paint. Water-based paints, such as artist or decorator acrylics, are a good choice. Free from solvents, they are relatively safe to use, and brushes can be cleaned with water.

Choosing a brush for the details

1 For the best results, apply paint to a primed surface. Choose a white primer if you want light-colored paints to appear bright and clear, and use a broad, soft brush to apply the paint smoothly and evenly.

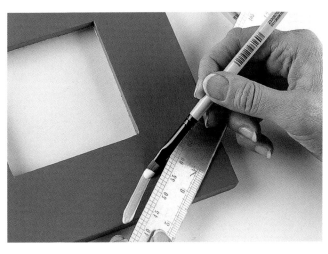

2 A flat brush is a good choice for painting broad lines. Use a ruler to steady the brush if you want the lines to be straight.

3 A pointed brush is good for painting fine lines and details. Lay the loaded brush flat against the surface to paint a neat flower petal.

4 For really fine lines, such as those on the Marbled Motif frame on pages 48–51, use a specialist brush called a rigger, which has long bristles.

Mats

A window mat is a rectangle of card cut to fit the frame, with an aperture cut into it to display the picture. Like frames, mats can be bought ready-cut, cut to your own specifications by a picture framer, or you can cut your own. However, cutting a beveled mat will require special equipment or a very steady and practiced hand with a craft knife and steel ruler, so it is best left to a professional.

Finishing a frame

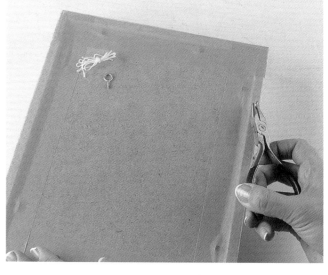

1 Once your frame has been decorated, replace the glass and place your chosen picture (and your mat, if using one) inside the frame.

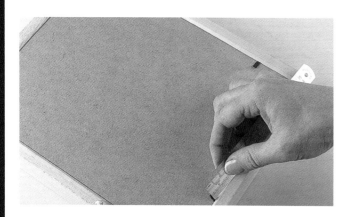

2 Replace the backing board and bend the flat metal pins down using small pliers or a hard, flat item such as a steel ruler.

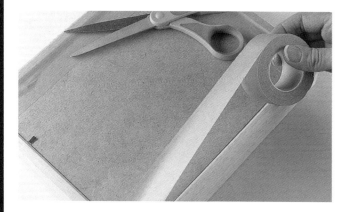

3 To seal the gaps between the backing board and the frame, cover them with strips of self-adhesive brown paper tape.

4 Insert screw eyes about one-quarter to one-third of the way down from the top, on either side of the frame (on the two long sides if the frame is to hang vertically, or the two short sides if the frame is to hang horizontally). Tie a length of strong picture cord between the two screws.

HANGING

There are various ways to display frames. The simplest way to hang a frame is to insert two screw eyes into the back, on either side, about one-quarter to one-third of the way down, stretching a length of cord or wire tightly between the two. You can then hang it from a nail or hook inserted into a wall, or from a picture rail.

Some frames are meant to be propped upright on a surface (such as a tabletop or sideboard) and will need a support at the back; others can be stood on a shelf, leaning against a wall.

Embossing sheet metal

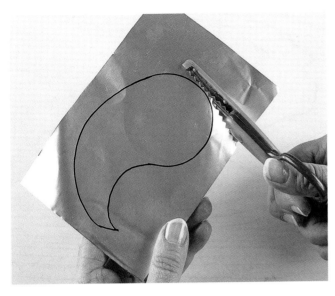

1 Cut metal to the size and shape you require, using scissors (with straight or decorative blades). Be careful of sharp edges.

2 You may wish to draw your design in pen before beginning to emboss. Use a permanent marker pen and draw on the wrong side of the metal sheet.

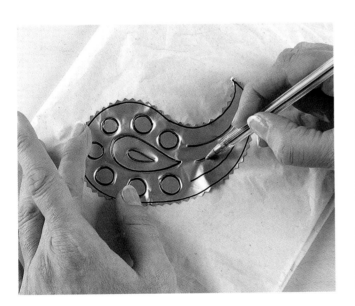

3 Place the metal sheet facedown on a pad of folded tissue or newspaper and, using a blunt instrument such as a ballpoint pen that has run out of ink or an embossing tool, trace over the lines using a little pressure so that the surface becomes indented.

4 You can impress further lines, dashes, or dots on this side or on the right side of the metal, if you wish, using the pen or a tracing wheel (as shown).

Making a rubber stamp

1 Draw your design on a scrap of craft foam (available from most craft stores). Try to make a shape that is simple.

2 Cut out the shape using scissors or a craft knife.

3 Apply glue (suitable for sticking foam rubber) to the reverse of the shape and stick it to a small block of wood, such as a child's building brick, and leave until the glue is dry.

4 To print, either press the stamp into a purchased ink stamp pad or coat the surface with poster paint or acrylic paint applied with a scrap of sponge or a roller.

Cutting and using a stencil

1 Draw or trace your chosen design onto a sheet of acetate film using a permanent marker pen.

2 Place the acetate on a cutting mat and carefully cut out the design using a scalpel or craft knife.

3 To hold the stencil in place while you apply paint, spray the wrong side of the stencil with a light coating of a semipermanent spray adhesive.

4 Using a blunt, stiff brush or a small piece of sponge, dab paint onto the cutout areas of the stencil. Leave to dry slightly before carefully lifting away the acetate to reveal your stenciled design.

Embroidering designs on fabric

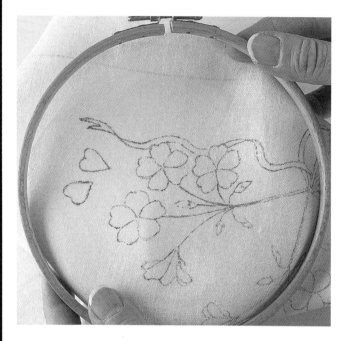

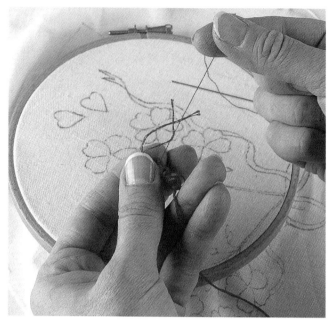

1 Draw your design on the fabric using a pen with waterproof ink if the lines are to be covered up by your stitches, or use a water-erasable or vanishing pen if you wish to remove the lines after embroidering. Stretch the fabric in a hoop or frame.

2 When using stranded embroidery thread, cut a length and then pull out single threads and use the appropriate-sized needle. Choose a crewel needle—one with a sharp point and a large eye.

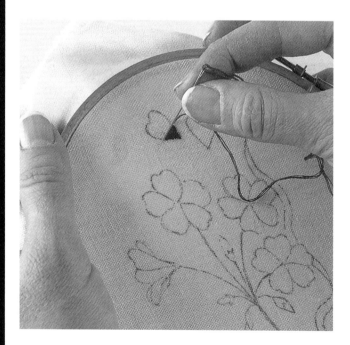

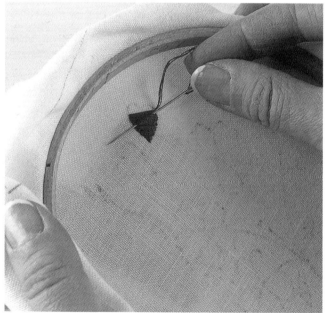

3 The best stitch for filling in shapes is satin stitch. Begin at one end of the shape to be filled and start making parallel stitches across the shape, close together so there is no fabric visible between them.

4 When you come to the end of a length of thread, run the needle under the stitches at the back of the work, then cut off excess thread.

Using simple fabric stitches

Lazy daisy stitch

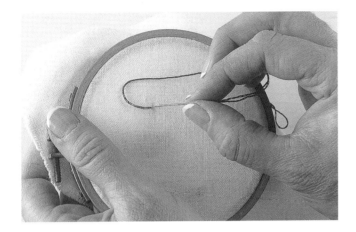

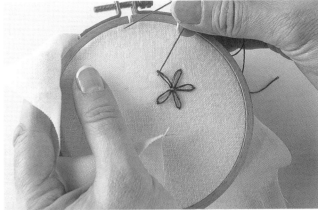

1 Start by bringing your needle up through the fabric at the point where you want the center of the flower. Push the needle back through the fabric, close to where you brought it out, leaving a loop of thread.

2 Bring the needle up again at the point where you want the tip of the flower petal, then push the needle back down, close to where you brought it out, trapping the loop underneath. Make four or five more looped stitches, in the same fashion, to complete the flower.

Blanket stitch

1 To stitch blanket stitch along the edge of a piece of fabric, bring the needle up through the fabric, a little way in from the edge, and insert it under the thread at the edge; repeat at even intervals.

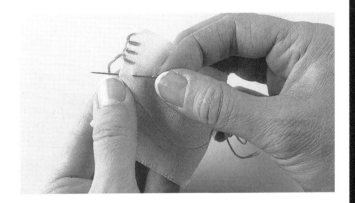

Boxes and albums

As with frames, your favorite craft, hobby, or stationery store will no doubt offer a wide range of boxes and albums ready for customizing.

Make sure the box you choose is made from sturdy cardboard to withstand the weight of a collection of photographs or other paraphernalia and is the right size to accommodate its contents. Boxes are available that are specially made to store photographs of a standard size (6 x 4 in.; 7 x 5 in.; 8 x 6 in. [15 x 10 cm; 18 x 12.5 cm; 20 x 15 cm respectively]; and so on), but

you may find that a sturdy shoe box or chocolate box does the job just as well—once decorated like the examples in the book, no one will know the difference.

Due to the phenomenal success of creating scrapbooks as a pastime, there is a wide selection of albums available. These can be bought ready-made or as individual components (covers, pages, and fastenings) in a range of stock sizes. The albums in this book have been made from scratch, but the techniques can easily be adapted to purchased albums if you prefer.

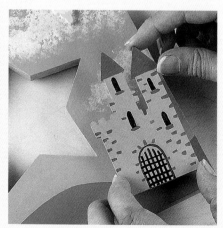

PAINTED AND
Patterned

Baby Days

This unusual frame was purchased at a thrift shop and given a new lease on life with a clever painted check pattern scattered with painted letters—perfect for displaying a baby photograph in the nursery. However, if you can't seem to find a frame, you can make one yourself from plywood or MDF (medium density fiberboard) if you are handy with woodworking tools.

Intermediate

You Will Need

- Old newspaper
- Frame measuring 11½ x 9½ in. (29 x 24 cm)
- Fine sandpaper
- Wooden letters
- White acrylic gesso primer
- Acrylic matte paints in white, golden yellow, lemon yellow, pink, light green, and orange
- Medium-sized flat paintbrush
- Masking tape, ¾ in. (2 cm) wide
- Cutting mat
- Metal ruler
- Craft knife
- Small, flat paintbrush
- Wood glue

1 Protect your work surface with old newspaper. Lightly sand the frame, especially if it has been painted or varnished. Also sand the letters if they have rough edges. Paint the frame and letters with two coats of primer, letting the first coat dry before applying the second. Paint the whole frame white.

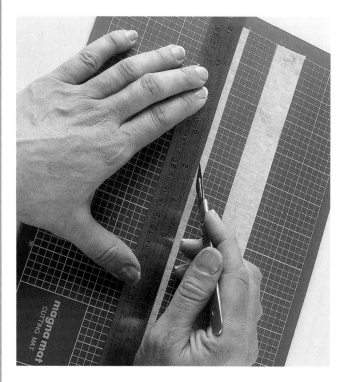

2 Lay strips of masking tape on the cutting mat and use the metal ruler and craft knife to cut into strips about ¼ in. (6 mm) wide x the length of your frame. Peel off and stick the strips vertically onto the frame, evenly spaced.

3 Paint stripes between the tape strips with a coat of white paint; leave to dry, then paint over with yellow. Leave to dry before peeling away and discarding the masking tape.

4 Paint the alphabet letters using the yellows, pink, green, and orange paints. Let dry while you prepare to paint the second set of stripes.

5 Stick strips of fresh masking tape, once again evenly spaced, but this time horizontally across the width of your frame.

6 Paint between the strips, using the pink paint. Leave to dry; then peel off the masking tape and discard it.

7 With the small, flat brush paint freehand stripes of light green down the centers of the pink stripes; then paint down the centers of the yellow stripes. If the idea of painting freehand stripes is too daunting, use a ruler as a guide.

HANDY HINTS

■ This is a cheerful color scheme suitable for a baby boy or girl. You could use other color combinations, perhaps to match a room decor.

■ Paint has a tendency to seep under the edge of masking tape. To ensure a crisp line, paint stripes in the background color first so that any seepage will not show. Leave to dry; then paint in your chosen color.

8 When all of the paint surfaces are thoroughly dry, stick the letters onto the frame with wood glue. Finally, insert the photographs into the frame.

Fabulous Fresco

Using modest materials, you can create a plaster-effect frame with pretty leaf and heart motifs dotted around the edges. The frame shown here is a standard size, designed to fit a 6 x 4-in. (15 x 10-cm) photograph, but the technique is easily adaptable to any flat frame. The method and materials should appeal to anyone who approves of recycling, because you can use cardboard shapes cut from a sturdy cardboard box, string, and the kind of tissue paper used by stores to wrap fragile items. The paints used here are free-flow acrylics. You can use any brand, mixing the colors yourself as instructed here, or buy premixed pastel colors.

Intermediate

You Will Need

- Old newspaper
- Plain flat wooden frame, 9½ x 7½ in. (24 x 19 cm), with an aperture of 5½ x 3½ in. (14 x 9 cm)
- Fine sandpaper
- 2B pencil
- Household glue
- Household string
- Thick cardboard scraps
- Scissors
- Wooden heart shape
- Tissue paper
- Free-flow acrylic paints in titanium white, cadmium yellow, process cyan, and process magenta
- Acrylic matte varnish

1 Protect your work surface with old newspaper. If the frame is coated with varnish or paint, you will need to sand the surface. Then, with a pencil, lightly mark the curving lines of the stem on the frame. Do this freehand; your pencil lines will be covered up later.

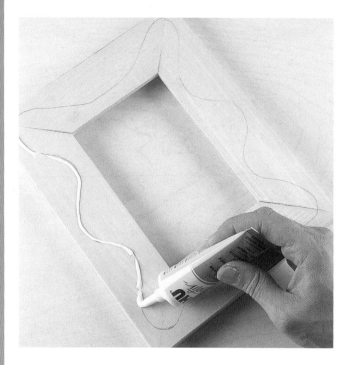

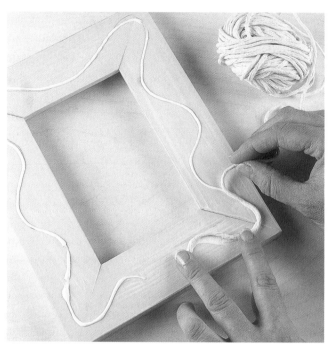

2 Carefully apply a trail of household glue over the pencil lines.

3 Neatly press the string in place over the lines of glue. Allow to dry.

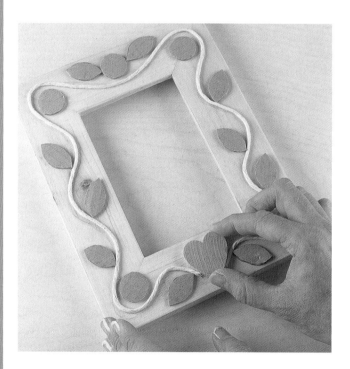

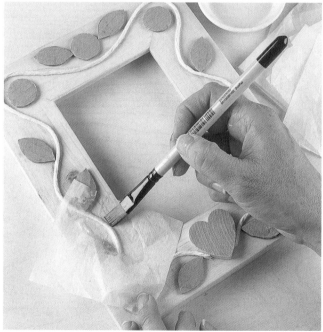

4 Draw 10 leaf shapes and 5 circles on scraps of thick cardboard and cut out. The leaves should be 1¼ x ¾ in. (3 x 2 cm) and the circles 1 in. (2.5 cm) across. Apply glue to the back of each shape and stick them on the frame, as shown. Stick down the wooden heart. (Wooden cutouts such as these are available from craft and hobby stores; if you cannot find them, cut your own from cardboard.) Let dry for about 20 minutes.

5 Dilute a small quantity of household glue with an equal quantity of water. Mix well and brush the mixture all over the frame, the string, and the added shapes, as shown. Apply torn pieces of tissue paper and push these into the crevices around the shapes, brushing with more glue as you go. Aim to cover the whole frame with two or three layers of tissue, then let dry overnight.

6 Mix titanium white with a dab of cadmium yellow paint to make a creamy yellow color and use this to paint the whole frame. You may need to apply a second coat. Let dry before applying additional coats of paint. Meanwhile, divide any leftover creamy yellow between two mixing plates.

HANDY HINT

You need to use household glue for this project. Use it undiluted for gluing cardboard and string in place, and diluted for the layers of papier mâché.

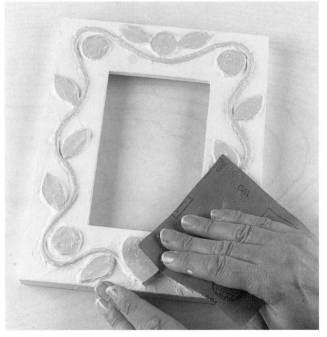

7 Add a dab of process cyan to one plate and a dab of process magenta to the other and mix well, adding more titanium white, if necessary, to make a pale green and a peachy pink. Use these colors to paint the stems and leaves green, and the circles and the heart pink. You may need to apply two coats. Let dry thoroughly.

8 To achieve a distressed effect, lightly sand the painted surface. Do not rub too hard. When you are satisfied with the result, protect the paint surface with two coats of acrylic matte varnish. Insert the photograph into the frame.

Childhood Treasures

A novelty frame is the basis for this pretty frame created to adorn a child's bedroom. With its castle motif it is fit for a princess. If the frame is for a boy, you could decorate it with a train or car. Feel free to use your imagination and create your own fantasy frame—it couldn't be easier. Novelty frames are not difficult to find, or if you wish, you could cut one—or get someone who is handy with a saw to cut one for you—using the star template on page 164. There you will also find templates for the wooden castle, flowers, and butterfly, though precut shapes are readily available from well-stocked craft stores.

Intermediate

You Will Need

- Old newspaper
- Frame, 9 x 7 in. (23 x 18 cm), with a star aperture
- Fine sandpaper
- White acrylic gesso primer
- 2B pencil
- Free-flow acrylic paints in titanium white, process cyan, lemon yellow, cadmium red, and mars black
- Medium and small paintbrushes
- Small sponge (natural or synthetic)
- Plywood shapes (or thick cardboard, see templates, page 164)
- Scissors
- Wood glue
- Hot-melt glue gun (optional)

1 Protect your work surface with old newspaper. Sand the frame and paint with two coats of primer, letting the first dry before applying the second.

2 Draw a wavy pencil line across the frame, close to the bottom edge. Mix cyan and white together to make a sky color and paint all over the frame above this line.

3 Add a little more cyan and some lemon yellow to the mixture and paint the grassy area below the line. Let dry.

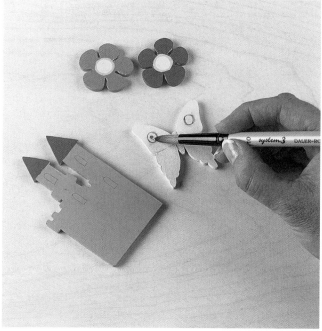

4 Dip the sponge into white paint, dab off any excess, and dab onto the frame to create clouds. Let dry. If you cannot find wooden cutouts, photocopy and cut out the castle, butterfly, and two flower templates on page 164. Then cut these out of thick cardboard.

5 Using a fine paintbrush and mixing colors where necessary to obtain the appropriate shades, (for example, mix white with a little black to make gray for the castle), paint the wooden or cardboard cutouts with as much or as little detail as you wish. Let dry.

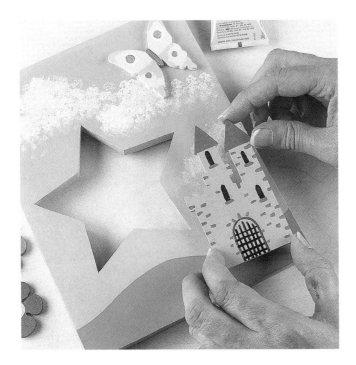

HANDY HINT

A fine artist's paintbrush will enable you to paint the shapes with small details. When using acrylic paints, rinse the brush in clean water between colors and, after you have finished painting, wash out any paint residue thoroughly. If you leave the paint to dry on the brush, it will harden and you will have to throw the brush away.

6 Stick the shapes in position on the frame using wood glue or a hot-melt glue gun.

COUNTRY ROAD

In this variation the frame has been turned sideways, but the same method has been used to create a colorful landscape for the painted cars.

Pet Friendly

Here is a fun frame for a photograph of your pet that combines a textured paint effect with bold, whimsical cutouts. A child could could help make this project, enjoying the messy spatter painting or using dextrous small fingers to cut out the more intricate shapes from craft foam. The motifs you need can be found on page 165.

The motifs you need can be found on page 165.

Easy

You Will Need

- Old newspaper
- Flat frame, 8¼ x 6¼ in. (21 x 16 cm), with an aperture of 6¼ x 4¼ in. (16 x 11 cm)
- Fine sandpaper
- White acrylic gesso primer
- Free-flow acrylic paints in titanium white, lemon yellow, and process cyan
- Medium-sized paintbrush
- Old toothbrush or bristle brush
- Dog and bone motifs (see page 165)
- Scrap cardboard
- Pencil
- Small craft scissors
- Craft foam in black and white
- Short length of narrow ribbon
- Goggle eyes
- Craft foam adhesive

1 Protect your work surface with plenty of old newspaper. Sand the frame and paint with two coats of primer, letting the first coat dry before applying the second. Mix a background color of deep green by combining equal quantities of cyan and lemon yellow. Brush this onto the frame, adding a second coat, if necessary, once the first coat is dry.

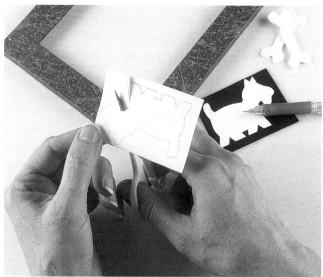

2 Mix cyan, yellow, and white in varying quantities to make shades of blue and green. Dip the toothbrush or bristle brush into one of the colors and draw the knife across the bristles so that the paint spatters onto the frame. Repeat with other colors until you have built up a richly textured surface. Let dry.

3 Meanwhile, photocopy or trace the motifs on page 165 onto cardboard and cut them out. Place the templates on the white craft foam and trace around them; then cut out the shapes. You will need six bones and one dog from white foam; one of the dogs should be cut from the black foam.

4 Use the narrow ribbon to make two dog collars, and stick the goggle eyes in position on each dog. Stick the shapes onto the frame, with the dogs facing each other at either of the bottom corners of the frame and the bones stuck down evenly around the frame. Let dry and mount the photograph.

FELINE FRIEND

For a cat, use the same method but cut out the cat and fish-bone motifs on page 165. You can also vary the color of the frame. Try a red background with spatterings of pink and orange, as here, or perhaps a black background spattered with white and shades of gray. Experiment on a piece of paper before you start work on the frame.

Aged Beauty

A plain wooden frame is given a special treatment to suggest weathered paint, with cracks revealing another color beneath, similar to the effect seen on old barn doors. This is easy to achieve with the right materials, but you will need to start with a plain wooden frame. The frame pictured here is wide, providing a generous painting surface. Any frame that has been painted or varnished will need to be lightly sanded with fine sandpaper before it is painted.

Easy

You Will Need

- Old newspaper
- Flat wooden frame, $10\frac{1}{2}$ x $8\frac{1}{2}$ in. (27 x 22 cm), with an aperture of $6\frac{1}{2}$ x $4\frac{3}{4}$ in. (17 x 12 cm)
- Fine sandpaper
- White acrylic gesso primer
- Matte latex household paints in pink and yellow
- 1-in. (2.5-cm) flat household paintbrush
- Crackle glaze (see Handy Hint, page 47)
- Acrylic varnish
- Metal embellishments
- Flat-headed nails (or panel pins)
- Hammer

Protect your work surface with old newspaper; then paint the whole frame with two coats of gesso primer, letting the first coat dry before applying the second. Then paint with two coats of pink. Let the paint dry.

2 When the pink paint is completely dry, brush on a coat of crackle glaze, working quickly and keeping your brushstrokes going in one direction only, according to the manufacturer's instructions. Let dry for 2 hours or the recommended time.

3 Paint a coat of yellow, with brushstrokes going in a different direction from the glaze; in other words, if you applied the glaze working from the top to the bottom of the frame, apply the yellow paint from side to side. Do not overwork the paint or you will disturb the glaze and spoil the effect. As the yellow paint dries, you will see cracks starting to appear. Leave overnight before applying two coats of acrylic varnish to protect the paint surface.

HANDY HINT

Cracked paint effects are not an exact science: There are a number of products available in stores, and the results vary. It's a good idea to practice the technique on a spare piece of wood and use different combinations of colors. Extreme color contrasts—such as red and dark green, navy blue and yellow, or chocolate brown and cream—often give the most dramatic results, but closer color combinations can also be really effective. Have fun experimenting!

4 As a final decorative touch, choose some metal embellishments, the kind sold for scrapbooking, and attach each of them to the frame with a flat-headed nail or panel pin hammered into the wood. Insert the photograph in the frame.

Marbled Motif

You can achieve impressive decorative results with just a little paint and a little patience. This marble effect is ideal for pictures of your ancestors, and you can vary the color scheme. You do not need to start with a frame exactly like the one pictured here. This effect would work well on a variety of frames and can be adapted for many different shapes and sizes. If you are attempting this type of effect for the first time, a frame with a smooth, flat, or curved surface is preferable.

Easy

You Will Need

- Old newspaper
- Plain wooden frame with a flat or curved profile, 9 x 7 in. (23 x 18 cm), with an aperture of 6¼ x 4½ in. (16 x 11 cm)
- Fine sandpaper
- White acrylic gesso primer
- Medium-sized paintbrush
- Free-flow acrylic paints in lemon yellow, titanium white, cadmium red, and cadmium yellow
- Mixing plate
- Small sponge
- Palette
- Rigger paintbrush or feather (see Handy Hint, page 51)
- Acrylic gloss varnish

1 Protect your work surface with old newspaper. If the frame is coated with varnish or paint, you will need to sand the surface.

2 Paint the whole frame with two coats of gesso primer, letting it dry between coats.

3 Next, paint the frame with a coat of lemon yellow and let dry.

4 Squeeze small blobs of lemon yellow and titanium white paint onto your mixing plate or palette. With the sponge, pick up a little white paint, remove the excess on the newspaper, and dab the sponge onto the surface of the frame. If the white paint begins to dominate, dab a little yellow over it. Work quickly because the next stage depends on this background still being slightly wet.

5 Squeeze a little cadmium red paint onto the palette and dip the tip of the rigger brush or feather into it, then drag it gently across the frame, making faint diagonal lines, as shown.

6 To soften the lines in places, dab gently with a clean corner of the sponge. Randomly apply a few white lines as well, still working quickly before the paint dries. Examine your work. If the lines still seem too dominant, you can always dab a little of the background colors over them to soften the effect. Dilute a little cadmium yellow with water and flick this onto the frame to create a spattered effect. Set the frame aside until the paint is completely dry.

HANDY HINT

A rigger paintbrush, so called because it is used to paint fine lines such as the rigging on sailing ships, is an ideal tool for creating fine, broken lines that look like marbled paint. If you do not wish to invest in this specialty brush, however, you can use a bird's feather: A goose feather is ideal and is often employed by paint experts.

7 Finally, seal the painted surface with two or more coats of gloss varnish. Let dry. Insert the photograph into the frame, using the desired mat.

Stamped Styles

Rubber stamps are a quick, easy, bold way to decorate a painted wooden frame. If you can't find the stamp you want from the many thousands available from stores, you can make your own. Here, stars and a stylized astrological symbol make a bright design to frame a picture of a new baby.

Easy

You Will Need

- Old newspaper
- Flat wooden frame, 10 in. (25.5 cm) square, with an aperture of 3¾ in. (9.5 cm)
- Fine sandpaper (optional)
- White acrylic gesso primer
- Soft paintbrush
- Masking tape
- Acrylic matte paints in green, blue, and red
- Paper mixing plate
- Rubber stamps (or see Handy Hint on page 54 for how to make your own)
- Craft foam
- Craft knife
- Acrylic varnish

1 There was no need to sand this frame, but if your frame has been painted or varnished, sand it lightly. Protect your work surface with old newspaper. Paint the whole frame with two coats of gesso primer, letting the first coat dry before applying the second. Then paint with two coats of green. Let dry.

2 Mask off the center of the frame, leaving a narrow ¼-in. (6-mm) border around the inner and outer edges. Paint the two borders, on the top part of the frame only, with green. This is to ensure a crisp edge once the masking tape is removed. Let dry.

3 When the green paint is dry, paint the borders in blue, making sure you paint the inner and outer edges of the frame as well. Let dry thoroughly before removing the masking tape.

4 Pour a small puddle of blue paint onto a mixing plate and dab the larger star stamp into it. Dab off any excess paint (the stamp should not be overloaded with paint). Carefully press the stamp onto each corner of the frame; then carefully lift it away. Repeat with the smaller star stamp, using red paint, and stamp a star in between each of the blue stars. Make a stamp of your chosen star sign and stamp this below the picture area.

HANDY HINT

To make your own stamp, trace your chosen design (the two star shapes and 12 zodiac symbols can be found on page 166) onto a piece of craft foam. Cut out the foam shape with scissors, and glue to a small block of wood. Wooden stamping blocks can be purchased from craft stores, but a child's wood playing block does the job just as well.

5 Let the paint dry thoroughly, then varnish with two coats of acrylic varnish. Let dry after each coat. Finally, insert a photograph into the frame.

PERFECT PUMPKIN

This smaller, square frame has been painted all over in a shade of purple with black borders. Two different stamps have been used. This dramatic decoration is the perfect border for a Halloween picture.

Trinkets and Treasures

A small box is a great storage place for treasured personal possessions, and you can make it special with a decorative stencil. A plain, sturdy box cries out for a little decorative treatment. Use a commercial stencil or, better still, make your own. Use just part of the stencil to adorn a small box or repeat it on a larger one. The secret of successful stenciling is not to use too much paint. Simply dip the tips of the bristles of your stencil brush into paint and dab off any excess before applying it to the stencil; the brush should be almost dry. Keep the brush upright and dab the paint on, gradually building up the color.

Intermediate

You Will Need

- Old newspaper
- Box, 6 in. (15 cm) square and 3 in. (7.5 cm) deep
- White acrylic gesso primer
- Free-flow acrylic paints in titanium white, process cyan, process magenta, and lemon yellow
- Medium-sized soft paintbrush
- 8½ x 11-in. sheet acetate

- Fine black permanent marker pen
- Cutting mat
- Steel ruler
- Craft knife
- Repositionable spray adhesive
- Paper mixing plate
- 2 small stencil brushes or sponge dabbers
- Acrylic varnish

1 Protect your work surface with old newspaper. Paint the outside of the box and lid with two coats of primer and let dry thoroughly. Then paint the outside of the box with one coat of titanium white acrylic. Let dry.

2 Meanwhile, prepare the stencil. Mark the design on page 167 onto the acetate. Place the acetate on a cutting mat and, using a steel ruler and craft knife, cut it into two separate pieces (one stencil for the lid of the box, the other for the sides). Now, using the craft knife, carefully cut out the designs (see Handy Hint).

3 Spray the reverse side of the larger stencil lightly with adhesive and place it in position on the box lid. Squeeze small blobs of all four paint colors onto a mixing plate. Dip the tip of the stencil brush or dabber into white paint, dab off the excess on a spare area of the plate, and dab a little white paint all over the design area, picking up more paint as needed. Dip the tip of the dabber into yellow and dab onto all the flower centers. Then dip into magenta paint and dab on the plate to mix slightly, forming a peachy color, and dab onto the stencil to fill in the flower petals.

HANDY HINT

When cutting the stencil, make sure you are using a sharp, new blade. Keep the acetate flat on the cutting surface at all times. Use the tip of the knife and rotate the acetate as you go. Keep to the lines of the design. Any additional cuts and slits in the acetate will allow paint to seep through and spoil the result. If you do make an unnecessary cut, it can be repaired by sticking a small piece of cellophane tape to the underside of the stencil.

4 When all the petals have been filled in, use the second brush to mix yellow and cyan for the leaves. Do not overmix the paint, and dab onto a spare area of the plate to get rid of any excess before applying to the stencil. Peel away the stencil carefully.

5 Repeat with the smaller stencil on the sides of the box. Finish by protecting the painted surfaces with a few coats of acrylic varnish, applied with a soft brush. Let dry. Insert the photograph into the frame.

FLOWER FRAME

This stencil can be used to decorate other things, too, such as this mat. White and paler mixes of color look particularly effective on a dark background. Conversely, rich, dark colors look stunning on lighter-colored mats. When stenciling, try to blend the colors as much as possible instead of applying solid blocks of color.

A Glass Act

Instead of decorating the border, why not decorate the glass? A swirling silver border provides a stylish touch to a chrome frame, ideal for displaying a black-and-white photograph. Sophisticated and elegant, the design is simply traced onto glass and decorated with silver metal leaf. Though this project is straightforward, you will need a steady hand. To enhance the silver effect, the background is colored in using spray paint for a smooth finish. When using spray paints, it is crucial to work in a well-ventilated area and to wear a protective face mask.

Advanced

You Will Need

- Tracing paper and pencil (optional)
- Silver-plated or chrome frame (with glass) measuring 11 x 9 in. (28 x 23 cm)
- Old newspaper
- Size (bonding agent)
- Fine artist's paintbrush
- Silver leaf metal
- Soft cloth
- Thick brush
- Masking tape
- Blue spray paint

1 Trace the design on page 168 onto tracing paper or make a photocopy. Remove the glass from the frame and tape the tracing or photocopy facedown on the glass.

2 Protect your work surface with old newspaper. Flip the glass over and work on the reverse. Trace over the design using the bonding agent and a fine paintbrush. Leave for 10 to 15 minutes or dry according to the manufacturer's instructions.

3 Lay silver leaf metal onto the design, overlapping where necessary and smoothing it down with a soft cloth.

4 Brush off any excess leaf with a thick brush and store it for future projects.

5 Still working on the reverse of the glass, mask off the central rectangle with masking tape and apply an even coat of spray paint. Let dry. Peel off the masking tape and remove the tracing. Place the glass in the frame, along with your chosen photograph.

School Spirit

As a way of preserving memories of school days, this blackboard frame gets full marks. Starting with a scrap of medium density fiberboard (MDF) or plywood left over from a home decorating project, you can create a durable surface on which you can write and draw with chalk for a temporary decoration, or, for a permanent finish, with a poster paint marker or blackboard paint (available in craft stores).

Easy

You Will Need

- Old newspaper
- ½-in. (1-cm)-thick medium density fiberboard (MDF) or plywood, 12 x 9 in. (30 x 23 cm)
- Universal primer
- 1-in. (2.5-cm) decorator's paintbrush
- Blackboard paint
- Fine sandpaper
- White artist's pencil
- Wood or household glue
- 2-in. (5-cm) colored matchsticks, 5 each in blue, red, yellow, and green
- White paint marker

1 Protect your work surface with old newspaper. Make sure the surface of the wood is clean, dry, and free from grease; then apply two coats of primer to one side of the wood and to the edges, letting the first coat dry before applying the second. Apply two coats of blackboard paint to the primed surface and edges for good coverage. Refer to the manufacturer's instructions: A light sanding between coats may be recommended; the instructions will also provide useful advice on drying times.

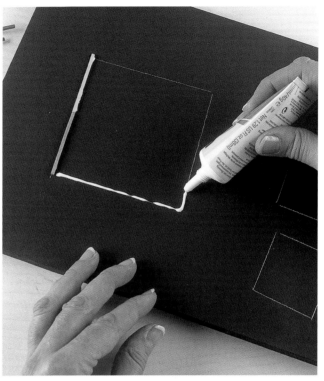

2 When the paint is completely dry, use the white artist's pencil to faintly draw a 4-in. (10-cm) square toward the top of the frame and three 2-in. (5-cm) squares in a row near the bottom.

3 Carefully apply a thin line of glue over the drawn lines and position the matchsticks over them. Let dry.

HANDY HINT

If you cannot find any colored matchsticks in your local craft store, make your own. Cut the burned tips from used matches, and paint each one with colored acrylic paints. Instead of matchsticks, you could use wooden Popsicle sticks or lengths of doweling.

4 With the paint marker, write and draw symbols in the spaces on the frame; you can copy the examples shown here or design your own, perhaps incorporating specific names and dates. Trim the photographs to size and affix them to the frame with wood glue.

DECORATED AND
Displayed

Traveler's Tale

Photos aren't the only way to preserve fond memories. If you have a particular vacation you want to display, why not frame a postcard? What's more, you can further enhance the image by using the map of the area as the frame. You will need two copies of the map, so it is best to work with color photocopies. This enables you to enlarge or reduce the scale as you desire. Any frame found in a thrift shop would be suitable, but those with a smooth surface, either flat or curved, will work best.

Easy

You Will Need

- Smooth, curved wooden frame
- 2 identical color photocopies of a map of your choice
- Scissors
- Paper glue
- Acrylic varnish
- Medium-sized paintbrush
- Mat board
- 2B pencil
- Cutting mat
- Craft knife
- Steel ruler

1 Cut one photocopy of the map so it is about 1 in. (2.5 cm) larger all around than the frame.

2 Protect your work surface with old newspaper. Cover the back of the map with paper glue and apply the glued surface to the front of the frame, making sure the map is placed centrally over it.

3 Cut out a rectangle from the center of the map, leaving a 1-in. (2.5-cm) border on either side of the frame. Snip diagonally into the inner corners of the frame, cutting right up to the corners, then fold down neatly around the inner opening of the frame to stick the paper down. Now make a diagonal cut at each outside corner of the frame. Smooth down the paper and fold neatly around the frame to stick it down.

HANDY HINT

A frame with a curved profile is particularly suitable for this technique, though a flat frame could be used with equal success. Using photocopies is ideal for incorporating antique maps into your framed memories. The map of Europe used in this project is a vintage one from 1951, perfect for displaying a contemporary photograph of one of London's most famous landmarks, Tower Bridge.

4 Brush a coat of acrylic varnish over the paper-covered frame. Let dry, then apply a second coat.

5 Meanwhile, make a matching mat. Centrally place the glass from the frame onto the second copy of the map. Draw around the glass using a pencil. Place on the cutting mat, then carefully cut out this rectangle using a craft knife and steel ruler and discard the rectangle (you will be left with the frame). Apply paper glue to the back of the map frame and place it, glued-side down, on a piece of mat board. Smooth down and leave until the glue is dry. Cut out an aperture slightly smaller than the size of your photograph. Trim off excess mat around the perimeter and tape your chosen picture to the back of the mat. The picture is now ready to be put into the frame.

FRENCH TWIST

In this example, a modern map of Paris and a plain ivory mat have been used to frame an antique postcard showing the Arc de Triomphe. A great way to frame a postcard from a well-loved relative.

Pomp and Circumstance

Create the perfect frame to celebrate a graduation. Here, a mix of papers stamped with the theme in mind evokes academic achievement and creates a rich effect that is perfect for framing a graduation photo. Many of the methods and materials used in other crafts, such as scrapbooking, can also be utilized in decorating picture frames. Pasting paper onto a surface is also a time-honored decorating method, known as découpage. In these days of printed media, computers, and photocopiers, it has never been easier to find or generate material for découpage. For this project you could photocopy actual books and manuscripts belonging to the student that reflect his or her personal interests. You will also find some motifs to copy on page 169.

You will also find some motifs to copy on page 169.

Intermediate

You Will Need

- Old newspaper
- Flat wooden frame, 10 in. (25.5 cm) square with a 3¾-in. (9.5-cm)-square aperture
- Scissors
- Various photocopies on ivory or cream-colored paper
- Medium-sized soft brush
- Découpage medium
- Rubber stamps
- Black-ink stamp pad
- Small metal frame plate
- Flat-headed nails (or panel pins)
- Hammer

1 If you are using a frame the same size as the one shown, cut the photocopies into 4-in. (10-cm) squares. Otherwise, cut squares that are slightly larger than the width of the frame so that the edges can be tucked over the sides of the frame. Place these on the frame, rearranging them until you are satisfied with the design.

2 Protect your work surface with old newspaper. Starting with the four side pieces, brush the back of each piece with découpage medium and set in position, then smooth the surface of the paper. Tuck the paper over the edge of the central aperture and around the outer edge of the frame.

3 When all four side pieces are in place, paste the four corner pieces in position. If you are adding paper cutouts, cut them now and paste them in place.

4 A border stamp is useful for emphasizing the central aperture: Here, a quarter-circle stamp has been used along its four outer corners; you could use a piece of craft foam cut to shape. (For tips on making your own rubber stamps, see Techniques page 24.)

5 When you are happy with the design, brush on several coats of découpage medium to seal your work. Refer to the manufacturer's instructions when deciding how many coats to apply; some recommend as many as 10 coats for a really professional finish. Attach the name plate using a hammer and nails, then insert your chosen photograph into the frame.

Stunning Showcase

Small objects can be displayed creatively in a box that is divided into sections and decorated to match the theme of the collection. Craft and hobby stores are ideal places to look for this type of box. Usually constructed from soft wood or balsa, these boxes can be decorated any way you like. Here, ordinary gift-wrapping paper is used to link the theme with a group of items. In memory of a lovely garden, gift wrap printed with flowers and grass makes a suitable backdrop for some miniature replicas of garden ornaments and some photographs, trimmed to fit the sections.

You Will Need

- Old newspaper
- Box with dividers, overall size approximately 12½ x 6½ in. (32 x 17 cm)
- White acrylic gesso primer (optional)
- Medium-sized soft brush
- Ruler
- 2 sheets gift-wrapping paper
- Scissors
- Découpage medium
- 12-in. (30-cm) floral braid
- Fabric glue
- Photographs
- Scraps of mat board
- Self-adhesive sticky pads (optional)

1 Protect your work surface with old newspaper. It is a good idea to paint unfinished wood with one or two coats of primer to help seal the surface. Let dry after each coat.

2 Measure the sections and cut pieces of gift wrap to fit. Concentrate on covering the larger surface first. Brush découpage medium on the reverse of the paper and press into place, smoothing out any air bubbles; use a fingernail, a plastic knife, or similar tool to push the paper into all the angles.

3 Cut small strips of paper to fit any gaps and stick them in place.

4 When the whole box is covered, seal the surface with a coat of découpage medium. Let dry, then brush on several more coats, letting each coat dry before applying the next. Cut two lengths of braid and glue along the central dividers.

5 Mount photographs on mat board and cut to fit some of the apertures. Push these into position. (If cut accurately to size, they will sit snugly at the back of the section and can be removed and replaced at a future date; otherwise, you may wish to glue them in position.) Add the objects or ornaments you wish to display once the box is in position. Use sticky pads to hold them in place, if desired.

Warm Welcome

The simplest of frames can be transformed with the help of glass paints and colored paper cutouts. Simple yet effective, this is a perfect gift for the parents or grandparents of a new baby. Made from a sheet of glass, a sheet of hardboard, and spring clips, a frame such as this is just begging for some creative treatment. Here, a paper collage frames a precious baby photograph, sandwiched between hardboard and glass and enhanced with outlines in black and silver on the glass itself. This is easy to make, but as effective as more sophisticated techniques.

Intermediate

You Will Need

- Old newspaper
- 8½ x 11-in. (A4) tracing paper (or make photocopies; see Handy Hint, page 80)
- 2B pencil
- 8½ x 11-in. (A4) blue paper
- Small, sharp scissors
- Craft paper in white, yellow, green, pink, orange, and violet
- 8½ x 11-in. (A4) clip frame
- Paper glue
- Relief paints for glass, in silver and black

1 Trace the design from page 170 twice onto tracing paper using a pencil, or make two photocopies using the mirror-image function on the photocopier (see Handy Hint, page 80).

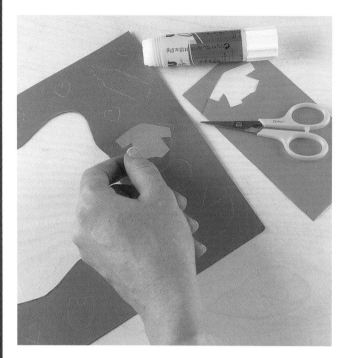

2 Protect your work surface with old newspaper. Trace the template onto the blue paper and cut out the aperture. Next, cut out the shapes from one of the copies and stick each one to a piece of colored paper, using the picture on page 78 as a guide (yellow for the teddy bear, pink and white for the feeding bottle, and so on). Cut out each shape carefully, using small, sharp scissors, and stick the colored-paper cutouts in place on the right side of this paper frame.

3 When all of the cutouts have been stuck down, place the glass on top and trace around the outlines using the silver relief paint.

HANDY HINT

This method uses a tracing or photocopy of the design stuck directly onto the colored paper to help you cut out the shapes accurately. Do not worry if the colored paper is very thin and the lines on the copies show through to the right side of the cutouts, because they will be covered up when you add the glass outliner.

4 Use the black relief paint to add extra details, such as the bear's features, the duckling's eye, and the markings on the bottle. Leave until completely dry, then add your chosen picture and insert the hardboard and clips.

Celebrations

The frame here features a colorful treatment that has a celebratory look. Scrapbooking is a popular hobby, and this frame is great for displaying one of those special pages you don't want to hide away in an album. Specially made to fit a 12-in. (30-cm) square page, the frame is sold unfinished so you can decorate it any way you like. You will no doubt find something similar in your local craft or hobby store. Here, a pasted paper border provides a colorful display case for a three-dimensional page. You can adapt the treatment for other parties and celebrations, such as Halloween, Thanksgiving, Christmas, and New Year's.

You Will Need

- Old newspaper
- Gift-wrapping paper in three coordinating designs
- Small, pointed scissors
- Découpage medium
- Medium-sized soft paintbrush
- Artist's pencils
- Frame, 14 in. (35.5 cm) square, to fit a 12-in. (30-cm) square scrapbook page
- 1 square 12-in. (30-cm) scrapbook page
- 1 square 12-in. (30-cm) mat board
- Double-sided sticky pads or silicone glue

1 Protect your work surface with old newspaper. Cut the wrapping paper into 12 rectangles, four of each color, each measuring 6 x 4 in. (15 x 10 cm). Brush découpage medium on the reverse of each one.

Maria

2 Stick the paper in place all around the sides, including the inner and outer edges of the frame. Smooth out with your fingertips.

3 Cut small scraps to paste over any gaps on the lower corners of the frame, which will be inconspicuous once the frame is on display.

4 Make color photocopies of the cupcake motifs on page 171. You will need 12 motifs. If you do not have access to a color copier, photocopy or trace the motifs, cut them out, then color in as desired using artist's pencils. Cut out each one carefully, using small scissors. Apply découpage medium to each motif and paste in place over the joins in the background paper.

HANDY HINT

When creating scrapbook pages, you should always use archival-quality materials, including acid-free papers and glues that will not stain the papers and photographs. It is also advisable to use only copies of your original photographs.

5 To protect the paper and provide a durable surface, coat the whole frame with several coats of découpage medium, letting each coat dry before adding the next. Mount the scrapbook page on mat board and secure to the frame using double-sided sticky pads or silicone glue.

MERRY MEMORIES

This treatment can be used on frames of any size. This 10-in. (25.5-cm) frame holds a 9-in. (23-cm) scrapbook page and has been decorated with Christmas wrapping paper, with the candy-cane motif photocopied from page 171. The depth of the box frame allows not only for 3D foam cutouts but also for the addition of a cluster of Christmas baubles in one corner, adding to the festive atmosphere.

Child's Photo Frame

Every child deserves a special, personalized frame. Colorful, whimsical, and easy to achieve, this project makes use of tiny pieces of childhood paraphernalia—the sort of things you'll find scattered on the floor, littering the desk, or lurking in the corners of drawers. Collect these tiny trinkets before they disappear up the vacuum cleaner, and put them to creative use. The frame pictured is wide enough to display objects up to approximately 2 in. (5 cm) in size (though many of the items used here are smaller than this) and provides a flat surface to make sticking down easy.

Easy

You Will Need

- Old newspaper
- Flat wooden frame, 8 in. (20 cm) square, with a 3¾-in. (9.5-cm) square aperture
- Fine sandpaper
- White acrylic gesso primer
- Paintbrush
- Masking tape (optional)
- Acrylic paints in lavender and white
- Eraser-tipped pencil
- Acrylic varnish
- Assortment of small plastic toys, numerals, and letters (see Handy Hint, page 87)
- All-purpose adhesive

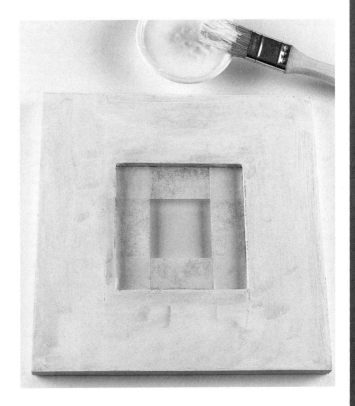

1 Protect your work surface with old newspaper. Any frame that has been painted or varnished will need to be lightly sanded with fine sandpaper before priming. In this frame the glass cannot be removed, so it has been protected with masking tape. Apply two coats of gesso primer, letting the first coat dry before applying the second.

2 Paint the whole frame lavender (or if this is for a boy, you could choose green, blue, or red). If you need to apply a second coat, allow the first coat to dry first.

3 Dip the eraser end of the pencil in white paint and dab spots evenly all over the frame, including the sides. Leave to dry before painting with a coat of acrylic varnish to protect the painted surface.

4 Arrange the small items all over the surface of the frame. When you are satisfied with the arrangement, glue them in place.

5 As a final decorative touch, glue the recipient's intitials and a couple of small toys to the top of the frame.

Notes to Remember

This elegant frame has a musical theme and an antiqued

finish, perfect for displaying a musical memory, such as a

concert playbill or an autographed photo of a favorite singer.

The frame shown here is flat with a slightly raised edge; a

completely flat frame would work just as well.

Advanced

You Will Need

- Flat frame, 10½ x 8½ in. (27 x 22 cm), with an aperture of 5½ x 3½ in. (14 x 9 cm)
- Sheet music manuscript
- Scissors
- Old newspaper
- Découpage medium
- Soft paintbrush
- 2-part crackle varnish (see Handy Hint, page 90)
- Artist's oil paint, in burnt sienna
- Soft rag

- Polyurethane varnish
- Sheet aluminum craft foil, at least 12 x 10 in. (30 x 25.5 cm)
- Cutting mat
- Steel ruler
- Craft knife
- Dressmaker's pattern wheel, old ballpoint pen, or embossing tool
- Adhesive suitable for metal foil
- Scrap cardboard, thin
- Self-adhesive sticky pads

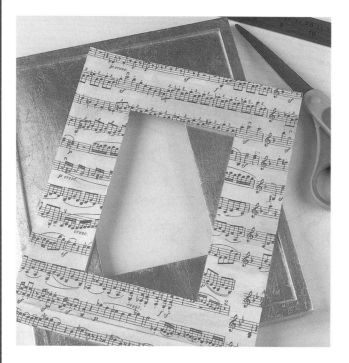

1 Make sure that the surface of the frame is clean, dry, and free from dust. Cut the music manuscript to fit the frame, cutting out a hole for the aperture, or, if this is too difficult, you could cut individual strips to fit each of the four sides.

2 Protect your work surface with old newspaper. Brush the reverse side of the paper with a generous coat of découpage medium and apply it to the frame. Smooth the paper, flattening out any wrinkles and air bubbles, and let dry. Brush on two coats of découpage medium over the whole surface to seal the paper, letting the first coat dry before applying the second.

3 Now brush on a thick coat of crackle varnish (see Handy Hint) and let dry thoroughly.

HANDY HINT

There are several brands of crackle varnish on the market, sold as a two-part product. If you can't find crackle varnish, use boiled linseed oil for the first product and glue size for the second product. This product is not to be confused with crackle glaze, which produces cracks and fissures on a painted surface.

4 Brush on a second coat of crackle varnish. The second coat needn't be as thick as the first. As it dries, you will see small cracks appearing in the varnish.

5 When the varnish is fully dry, smear burnt sienna oil paint over the entire surface of the frame with a soft rag, making sure to rub the paint into the cracks with the rag.

6 With a clean rag, continue to rub, removing the excess paint from the surface; a residue of paint will be left in the cracks. Protect the surface with several coats of polyurethane varnish applied with a brush and let dry.

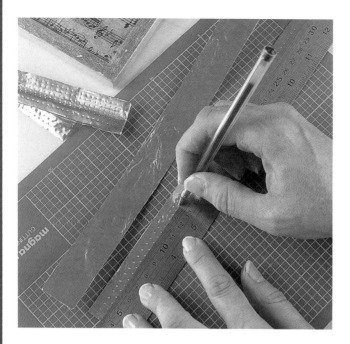

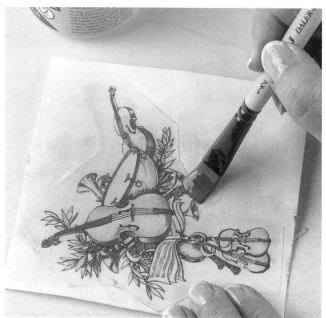

7 Meanwhile, make the border. Using the steel ruler and craft knife, cut strips of aluminum craft foil on the cutting mat. You will need two 10¹/₂-in. (27-cm) strips and two 8¹/₂-in. (22-cm) strips, each of them 1 in. (2.5 cm) wide, or wide enough to create a ³/₈-in. (1-cm) border and cover the edges of the frame. Create a pattern of dots by running a dressmaker's pattern wheel along the metal strips (or use an old ballpoint pen or embossing tool), then fold each strip in half lengthwise and glue to the frame.

8 For a final flourish, photocopy one of the images on page 165 and paste it to a piece of scrap cardboard using découpage medium. Apply two or three coats of découpage medium to the front and back of the cardboard, letting each coat dry before applying the next. Apply the two-part crackle varnish to the scrap and rub with oil paint, as before; then cut out the picture carefully. Apply self-adhesive pads to the reverse side of the cutout. Remove the protective backing from the pads and stick the cutout to one of the top corners of the frame. Insert your chosen photograph into the frame.

FOOD FOR THOUGHT

This frame is reminiscent of a Mexican artisan product. Made in exactly the same way as the manuscript frame, it is decorated with photocopies of food packaging. Look in your pantry and select products that have colorful packaging—breakfast cereals, soups, or even tortillas—and make color photocopies of them. Cut out the parts you like best and paste them onto a flat frame. Then follow Steps 3 through 8.

Mini Album

A small collection comprising a few precious photographs or perhaps some ticket stubs or postage stamps requires a small-scale album like this. There are so many pretty papers available, giving you an almost infinite scope for decoration. Combine stripes and florals, as here, or spots and squiggles, animal prints, and even nursery prints—it's up to you. Make one for yourself and lots more for friends and family.

You Will Need

- 8½ x 11 in. (A4) printed paper in two contrasting patterns
- Cutting mat
- Craft knife
- Steel ruler
- Household glue
- 2 pieces of mat card, each 6½ x 4½ in. (16.5 cm x 11.5 cm)
- Pencil
- Piercing tool
- ¾-in. (2-cm) button
- Darning needle
- Embroidery cotton
- Plain paper cut into pieces 10½ x 4¼ in. (26.5 x 11 cm)
- Photograph, 2 in. (5 cm) square
- Scrap of colored card
- 10-in. (25-cm) narrow ribbon

1 Choose a printed sheet of paper as the dominant pattern and cut the sheet in half across its width. Cut a strip measuring 5³/₄ x 2¹/₄ in. (14.5 x 6 cm) from the contrast paper. Apply a thin strip of glue along the two long edges of the strip and stick one half of the main paper on either side.

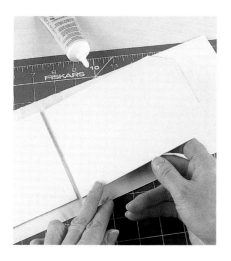

2 Place the prepared paper wrong-side up. Cut off two of the corners from each rectangle of cardboard, as shown. Apply a thin layer of glue to one side of each of the two cardboard pieces and place these glue-side down onto the paper, with a narrow gap of approximately $1/5$ in. (4 mm) in between.

3 Draw a $5/8$-in. (15-mm) border around the cardboard pieces and cut around this line. Apply glue and fold in the borders. Place the album on the contrast paper and draw around it with a pencil. Draw another line $1/5$ in. (4 mm) inside the first line and cut along this line. Apply glue to the reverse of the contrast paper and stick onto the inside of the album.

4 Cut two pieces of contrast paper, each 3 x $1^1/2$ in. (7.5 x 4 cm). Apply glue to half of each piece and stick to the front and back covers at the centers of the shortest edges. On the front piece pierce two holes to correspond with the holes in the button, and on the back piece pierce one hole. Stitch the button in place. Pass an 8-in. (20-cm) length of thread through the hole in the back and secure inside the album. Glue two small pieces of the main paper together and cut out a tiny label shape. Thread the end of the embroidery cotton through and knot the end.

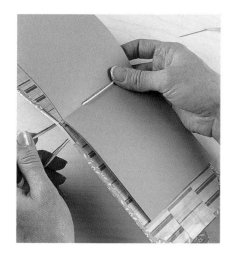

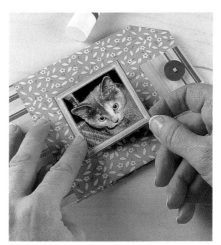

5 Glue the other half of each front and back flap to the inside of the album, covering up the thread ends. Then fold the plain paper pieces in half to form pages and stitch through the spine using several different threads and tying the ends in a firm knot on the outside.

6 Stick the photograph to a scrap of colored paper and stick down a border of narrow ribbon. Trim close to the outer edges of the ribbon and stick to the center of the front cover.

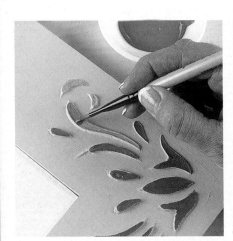

ADORNED AND
Bejeweled

Candy and Glitter

Crafters keen on recycling will be pleased to know
that this project utilizes colored foils saved from
chocolates and candy bars. The jeweled
embellishments are inexpensive faux gems
purchased from a craft or toy store. You could even
recycle old costume jewelry, such as a broken
necklace or brooch, or search through your button
box for sparkly specimens.

Easy

You Will Need

- Colored-foil candy wrappers

- Scissors

- MDF (medium density fiberboard)
  or plywood frame (see Handy Hint,
  page 100), 12 x 8¼ in. (30 x 20.5 cm),
  with an aperture of 7½ x 4½ in.
  (19.5 x 11.5 cm)

- Glue spreader

- Craft-foil adhesive

- Sequin strip to fit frame aperture

- Assortment of flat-backed gems

1 Gently crumple the candy wrappers and smooth
them out again. Cut the wrappers into manageable
pieces, large enough to wrap around the front and
sides of the frame and onto the back, with a margin
of about ¹/2 in. (12 mm).

HANDY HINT

You may find a similarly shaped
frame in a craft store—a number of
manufacturers sell MDF and plywood
blanks that are ready to decorate—
although a competent carpenter or
handyman can easily cut one from
1/4-in. (6-mm) or 1/2-in. (12-mm) MDF
or plywood. Alternatively, you could
cut one from foam board, which can
easily be cut using a craft knife. You
will find a template for the frame on
page 172. Cut one shape with an
aperture for the front and one without
an aperture for the back.

2 Using a glue spreader, apply craft-foil adhesive to
the reverse side of each candy wrapper and stick
them in place, overlapping the edges slightly so that
no wood shows through.

3 Glue the sequin strip to form a border around
the edges of the central aperture.

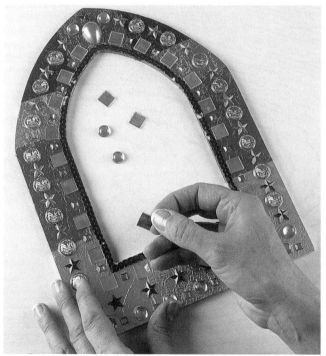

4 Place jewels over the frame in a symmetrical
pattern, arranging and rearranging them until
you are satisfied with the design. Glue the jewels
to the frame.

5 Cover the backing of the frame with wrappers, making sure to cut the pieces big enough to wrap around the sides. Place a picture in the center; then glue the two halves of the frame together.

DAZZLING DELIGHT

This treatment works well on flat frames of any shape or size. Here, a square frame has been covered with red foil and covered with an assortment of gems and sequins, stuck down close together in a random pattern for maximum impact and sparkle. This would be an ideal project to do with a child. Just make sure you use a solvent-free adhesive.

Custom Corners

A subtle three-dimensional pattern on a simple wooden frame is the perfect setting for a faded old photograph or a treasured watercolor sketch. The ideal frame for this project is flat and square, with a wide surface area that provides enough space for stenciling. The frame shown here has a small aperture, just 3½ in. (9 cm) square. Choose a small faded photograph, a subtle watercolor sketch, or any picture with pale colors to balance the delicate treatment of the frame.

You Will Need

- 8½ x 11-in. sheet acetate
- Fine black permanent marker pen
- Cutting mat
- Craft knife
- Spray adhesive
- Flat wooden frame, 10 in. (25.5 cm) square, with a 3½-in. (9-cm) square aperture
- Old newspaper
- Palette knife
- Relief stencil paste
- Fine sandpaper
- White acrylic gesso primer
- Free-flow acrylic paints in titanium white, green, lemon yellow, and crimson
- Soft medium-sized paintbrush
- Acrylic varnish

1 To prepare the stencil, trace the design from page 173 onto the acetate using the permanent marker pen. Place the acetate on a cutting mat and, using the craft knife, carefully cut out the design (see Handy Hint, page 105, for cutting tips). Spray the reverse side of the stencil lightly with the adhesive and place in position on one corner of the frame.

2 Protect your work surface with old newspaper. With the tip of the palette knife, scoop out a generous amount of stencil paste (the equivalent of about 1 tablespoonful) and place it onto the stencil. Spread it out to create an even, smooth layer no more than $1/4$ in. (6 mm) thick.

3 Carefully lift the stencil away from the frame; you will be left with a relief design. Repeat on the opposite corner and set the frame aside for 24 hours (or the time recommended by the manufacturer) to let the paste dry. Lightly sand the surface of the raised areas.

4 Paint the whole frame with a coat of gesso primer and allow to dry completely.

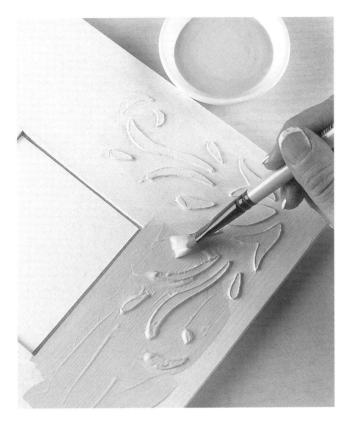

5 Now paint the frame with a coat of pale green (made by mixing titanium white with a little green and lemon yellow). Allow to dry between coats.

6 When the background color is dry, paint the flowers pink (using a mix of titanium white and crimson) and the leaves and stems green (with a mix of green and a little white). Protect the painted surface with several coats of varnish. Let dry between coats. Insert a photograph into the frame.

HANDY HINT

You will need to lift the stencil carefully to avoid smudging or dislodging the paste. If you do smudge it, simply wipe away the stencil paste immediately, make sure the surface of the frame is clean and dry, and start again. Immediately after stenciling, the paste is soft and vulnerable to damage, so put the frame in a safe place until the paste is dry and ready to be painted.

Tiled Treasures

Pictures are not the only things you can frame. Sometimes a three-dimensional object—a plaque or a prize rosette—looks great displayed on a wall. This frame is suitable for hanging in a humid environment, such as a steamy kitchen or bathroom, or even outside on a sheltered patio or porch. If you are new to mosaics, buy them ready-cut from larger craft stores; after you gain confidence in handling the materials, you can cut your own. In this project, whole and quarter mosaics have been used to great effect.

Advanced

You Will Need

- Old newspaper
- Wooden frame, 12 in. (30.5 cm) square
- Hardboard, 12 in. (30.5 cm) square
- Wood glue
- Small hacksaw
- 22 in. (56 cm) x ¼-in (6-mm) square section of soft wood
- Medium-sized paintbrush
- White acrylic gesso primer
- White acrylic paint
- Glass mosaic tiles: 72 whole ¾-in. (2-cm) tiles and 56 quarter tiles
- Tile adhesive
- White tile grout
- Palette knife
- Damp cloth
- Soft, dry cloth
- Abrasive household cleaner

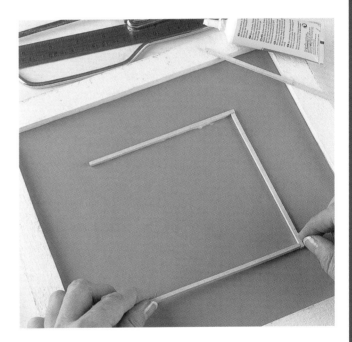

1 Protect your work surface with old newspaper. Glue the hardboard to the back of the frame with wood glue. With a small hacksaw, cut four 5½-in. (14-cm) lengths of square-section wood and place in the center of the hardboard to form an inner frame. Make sure that your tiles will fit between this and the edge of the frame, then glue the wooden pieces in place. Let dry. Paint the outer and inner frames with two coats of gesso primer, followed by two coats of white acrylic paint, ensuring that each coat is dry before applying the next.

2 Before sticking the tiles into position, place them in the frame, rearranging them, if necessary, until you are pleased with the design. Apply tile adhesive to the back of each quarter tile in turn before pressing it into place, pushing one edge against the inner frame and ensuring that there is a small gap between each tile for the grout.

3 Next, stick the outer border of tiles in place, pressing each tile against the edge of the frame and leaving a small gap between each tile. In the gap between the inner row of tiles and the outer border of the frame, stick the remaining tiles. Leave until the glue is completely dry and the tiles are stuck firmly in place.

4 Mix the grout (or stir it, if it is ready-mixed) and, using a palette knife or other suitable implement, spread a layer over the tiles, pushing it well into the gaps between the tiles.

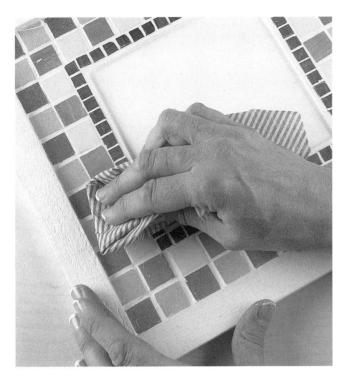

5 After all the gaps are filled, remove any excess grout from the surface of the tiles with the palette knife. Then wipe away any residue with a damp (not wet) cloth, taking care not to lift the grout from between the tiles. Once the grout is completely dry (allow 24 hours), polish the surface of the tiles with a soft, dry cloth. At this stage any stubborn bits of grout can be removed with the corner of a damp cloth and a little abrasive household cleaner if necessary. Mount your chosen object in the frame.

MORE ON MOSAICS

Once you feel confident about handling mosaic tiles, you can cut whole tiles into smaller pieces using a tile cutter. You should always wear protective eyewear when doing this. Here are two frames with narrow recesses that have been filled with cut tiles in a range of bright colors to form attractive striped patterns.

Fun and Fancy

Colorful and full of character, this square frame is an ideal surround for a happy photograph, such as a trip to the circus or of a child transformed with face paints—and who would guess that it is made with Popsicle sticks? This method, using colored sticks, produces a great finish with very little outlay or effort. Choose a plain wooden frame as a base, preferably one that has a flat indented area in which to place the wooden strips. Wooden Popsicle sticks are available plain or colored from most craft stores, or you could save the stick each time you eat a Popsicle, then color them yourself using paints or wood dyes.

Intermediate

You Will Need

- Old newspaper
- Wooden frame, 11 in. (28 cm) square, with an aperture of 8 in. (20 cm) square
- Fine sandpaper (optional)
- Damp cloth
- White acrylic gesso primer
- Medium-sized paintbrush
- Acrylic paints, in cadmium red, green, and white
- Flat artist's brush
- Flat, wooden Popsicle sticks in varying widths and colors
- Small hacksaw
- Vice or clamp (optional)
- Fine sandpaper
- Wood glue or household glue
- Acrylic varnish

1 Protect your work surface with old newspaper. If the frame has a painted or varnished surface, or if it is made of untreated wood but has a rough surface, lightly sand it all over. Wipe with a damp cloth to remove any dust or residue. Brush on one or two coats of gesso primer, letting the first coat dry before applying a second.

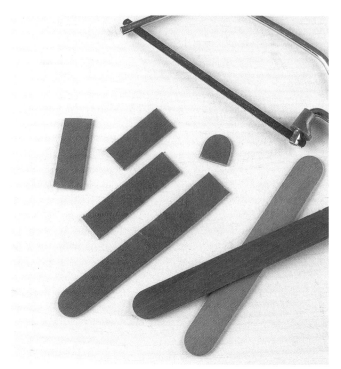

2 Use the cadmium red paint straight from the tube or pot or mix in a little white before applying it to the inner edges of the frame. Using the flat artist's brush, paint the outer edges in green, again with a little white mixed in if you wish. You do not need to be too neat where the colors overlap, because the wooden strips will cover up this central area.

3 Cut the Popsicle sticks into varying lengths. For the best visual effect, you will need at least seven or eight different colors. To cut the sticks, you will need to use a small hacksaw. It is advisable to hold each stick in a vice or clamp secured to a workbench before cutting it, and sand the cut edge with fine sandpaper to smooth any rough edges and avoid splinters.

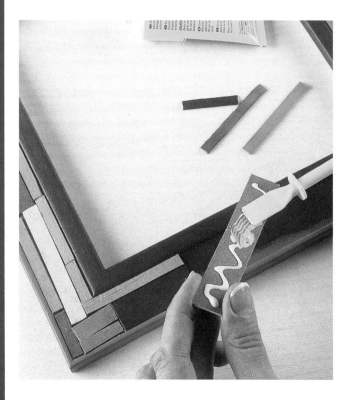

4 Use wood glue or household glue to stick down the sticks, making sure that there are no large gaps between each piece and that adjacent sticks are not of the same color. To protect the surface, apply one or more coats of varnish, letting it dry between coats. Insert your chosen photograph into the frame.

ADORNED AND BEJEWELED

Ocean's Edge

A scattering of sand and tiny seashells encrust this simple frame, perfect as a memento of a day on the beach or for displaying a single seashell or a photograph of a beautiful sunset. Look for a suitable frame with a flat surface. Bags or boxes of small shells are often sold for flower arranging or for decorating the home or garden, as well as for craft projects, so look in garden centers or home-furnishing stores as well as hobby stores for suitable shells. Of course, you can always collect your own seashells from the beach. Choose small specimens and collect only enough to complete the project, because sustainability is an issue. While you are there, collect a cupful of sand to fill in the spaces between the shells.

Easy

You Will Need

- Old newspaper
- Plain, flat wooden frame, $10^1/2$ x $8^1/2$ in. (27 x 22 cm)
- Assorted small seashells
- Household glue
- Small flat-bladed knife or glue spreader
- Sand

1 Protect your work surface with old newspaper. Before sticking the shells in position, place them on the frame to check positioning and spacing. Apply a generous layer of household glue over a small area of the frame—it is best to work in small sections at a time.

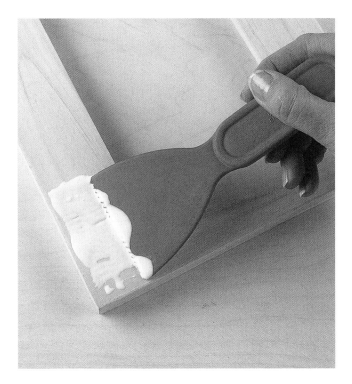

2 Using a flat-bladed knife or glue spreader, spread the glue evenly over the small section of frame.

3 Start by sticking down one or two of the larger shells from your selection, then add smaller ones, keeping them close together.

4 Gradually add more glue and continue sticking down shells, pushing them closely together until the whole frame is covered.

5 Before the glue starts to dry, sprinkle the whole frame with sand so that it fills all of the gaps between the shells. Leave until the glue dries completely before tipping the frame to get rid of excess sand. Insert your chosen photograph into the frame.

A Clear Case

Instead of consigning empty compact disc cases to the trash, why not do your part for the environment and recycle them into mini picture frames? CDs are an everyday presence, and the cases in which they are sold are, more or less, a throwaway item. These can be transformed into cute frames, however. The cases vary in construction, but most can be bent back on their hinges and will stand up with no extra support. Try doing this before you start decorating; you may need to take the case apart and reverse one of the pieces to get it to stand up. You will also need to remove the inner piece that holds the CD. This is a frivolous project, so do not aim for a sophisticated result. Instead, have fun with stickers, cutouts, fake gems, sequins, and dimensional paints. Treat it like a scrapbook page in miniature. Get the kids to join in; they will enjoy creating their own personalized picture frame in next to no time.

Easy

You Will Need

- Empty CD case
- Decorative cardstock, 5 x 4³/4 in. (12.5 x 12 cm)
- Steel ruler
- Pencil
- Cutting mat
- Craft knife
- Self-adhesive ribbon, ¹/2 in. (1 cm) wide
- Domed crystal stickers (see Handy Hint, page 118)
- Gift wrap with small repeat design
- Double-sided tape

1 Once you have cut a rectangle of decorative cardstock to size, check that it fits neatly and snugly into the lid of the CD case. Measure and mark an aperture of 2¹/4 in. x 2 in. (5.5 x 5 cm) centrally on the back of the card.

2 Place the card facedown on the cutting mat and cut out the aperture using a steel ruler and a craft knife.

3 Cut four lengths of ribbon slightly longer than the four sides of the aperture. Peel off the backing and lay each one onto the card. To miter the corners for a neat finish, lay the ruler diagonally across the corner of the ribbon and cut away excess with the craft knife.

HANDY HINT

Domed stickers for cardmaking and scrapbook projects are sold in craft stores. Variously labeled, they are simply domed circles of acrylic with a self-adhesive back, available in a range of sizes. Choose a package of assorted sizes for this project.

4 Place the domed stickers over individual designs on the wrapping paper. Cut each one out roughly, leaving a small margin of paper all around. Apply a piece of double-sided tape to the back of each one and then cut neatly around the sticker.

5 Arrange the stickers on the front of the card in a pleasing pattern. Peel off the backing of the tape and stick each one in place. Apply strips of double-sided tape to the back of the card and stick in place on the CD cover. Stick your chosen picture to the reverse of the cover so that it can be viewed through the aperture.

COVER STORIES

Have fun experimenting with various materials. You may wish to create a theme that is reflective of the picture displayed within. For example, stick on miniature tools for a photo of a do-it-yourself enthusiast or flowers for a gardener.

Lasting Impressions

This embossed metal frame is relatively easy to make and calls for no special skills, yet the effect is dazzling. Soft metal foil with a simple repeat pattern is further enhanced with fake "diamonds," making this the perfect gift for a silver or diamond wedding anniversary. It would also make an ideal frame for a treasured portrait. For the best effect, choose a frame that is quite deep. A wooden or metal frame would be suitable; it does not matter if it is scratched, chipped, or otherwise damaged, because the foil will cover the original surface completely.

You Will Need

- Flat frame, 9¼ x 7 in. (23.5 x 18 cm), with an aperture of 5½ x 3½ in. (14 x 9 cm)
- Aluminum craft foil in silver or gold
- Steel ruler
- Embossing tool or old ballpoint pen
- Scissors
- Old newspaper
- Adhesive suitable for metal foil
- Small cup or jar
- Scissors with decorative blades
- 10 fake "diamonds"

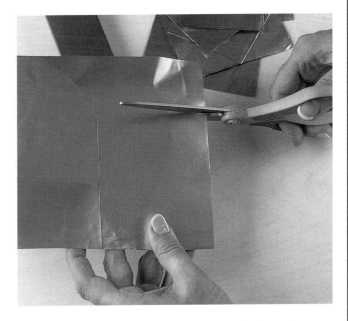

1 Cut rectangles of aluminum foil to fit the sides, top, and bottom of the frame. In this case, the depth of the aperture is ³/₈ in. (1 cm) and the sides of the frame are ³/₄ in. (2 cm) thick. Allowing for some overlap at the back, the pieces you cut will measure 5¹/₂ x 3¹/₂ in. (14 x 9 cm) for each side, 3¹/₂ x 3¹/₂ in. (9 x 9 cm) for the top and bottom, and four corner pieces each 3¹/₄ in. (8 cm) square. To measure and cut the pieces, use a steel ruler and score along the lines to be cut with the embossing tool or an old ballpoint pen. Cut along these lines with scissors.

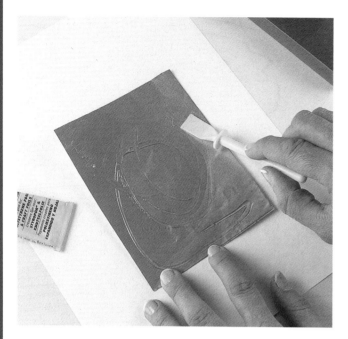

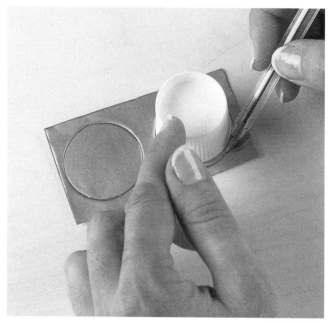

2 Protect your work surface with old newspaper. Following the manufacturer's instructions, apply adhesive to the reverse of each foil piece and to the frame, wait 10 minutes (or the recommended time), and then press each piece in place, starting with one of the side pieces. Press the second side piece in place, then the top and bottom pieces. Position the corner pieces so they slightly overlap the pieces already stuck down.

3 Choose a round object, such as a small cup or jar, with a diameter of approximately 1¹/₂ in. (4 cm) as a template. Place your template on a piece of foil and draw around it using the embossing tool or the ballpoint pen. Repeat this step nine more times.

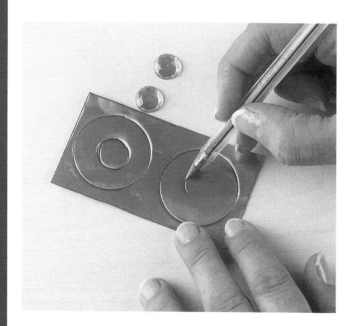

4 On each circle draw an inner circle slightly larger than the "diamond" (you can draw around the spot where you will position the "diamond," or just draw a circle freehand as shown).

5 Still using the ballpoint pen, draw lines radiating out from the inner to the outer circle, likes spokes on a wheel. Using scissors with decorative blades, cut out around the edge of each circle.

6 Now apply glue to the reverse of each foil disk (the side with the indentations) and on the frame, where each is to be stuck. Leave the glue for 10 minutes (or the recommended time) and press the foil disks into position.

7 Finally, using the same glue, stick a "diamond" in the center of each circle. Insert your chosen photograph into the frame.

HANDY HINT

Foil is sometimes available in different sizes. For this project, small sheets are ideal. Save any scraps for future projects. The foil is available in a range of metal finishes; sometimes it is silver-colored on one side and gold- or brass-colored on the other, so if you are making this project for a golden wedding anniversary gift, you may want to choose a gold finish.

Love Letters

Here is a small box that is perfect for storing letters or postcards. The lid is covered with paper that is decorated with lines of handwriting—look for suitable gift-wrapping paper or photocopy an old letter—and decorate it with an embossed metal frame in which you can place a little pictorial clue to the contents within.

You Will Need

- Box with lid, measuring approximately 7 x 5 in. (18 x 12.5 cm)
- Gift-wrap paper with script
- Steel ruler
- Pencil
- Scissors
- Old newspaper
- Paper adhesive
- Aluminum craft foil in silver or gold
- Embossing tool or old ballpoint pen
- Scissors with decorative blades
- Hole punch
- Piercing tool or awl
- Adhesive suitable for metal foil
- 4 paper brads

1 Place the box lid upside down on the wrapping paper and, placing a ruler up against the edge of the lid, draw a pencil line all around. Cut along this line using the straight scissors.

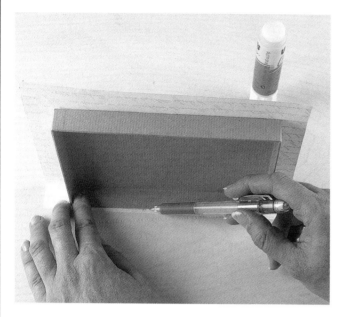

2 Protect your work surface with old newspaper. Spread paper adhesive over the top surface of the box lid and place it centrally on the wrong side of the wrapping paper. Fold the edges over the sides of the lid and draw along each edge, onto the paper, as shown. Trim off excess with scissors. Apply paper adhesive to the edges of the paper and press in place, folding the corners for a neat result.

3 Trace or photocopy the plaque design on page 173. Tape it to the wrong side of a piece of aluminum craft foil. If the foil is silver-colored on one side and gold on the other, you can choose which side should be the "right" side.

4 Go over the lines with an embossing tool or an old ballpoint pen, pressing lightly and using a ruler to help keep the lines straight. Remove the paper and, if necessary, go over the lines again. Try not to press too hard or you may make holes in the foil. The aim is to make clear embossed lines. Use the tip of the tool or pen to press dots into the foil at the corners, where indicated.

5 Using scissors with decorative blades, cut out the plaque. Then punch a hole in each of the four corners. These holes are where the paper brads will be inserted.

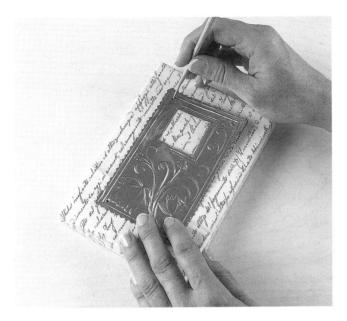

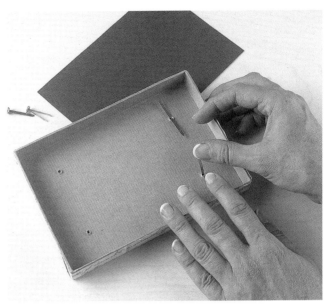

6 Place the plaque centrally on the box lid and mark the positions of the four holes. Use an awl to pierce holes in the box lid.

7 Choose a picture to place in the aperture. If this is to be permanent, you can glue it in place on the box lid or on the back of the plaque, then glue the plaque in place using the foil adhesive before inserting the paper brads. If you think you might wish to change the picture, tape it to the plaque and do not glue it to the box, but simply hold it in place with the paper brads.

HANDY HINTS

- To cover the ends of the paper brads, cut a piece of craft paper to fit the inside of the box lid and glue in place or hold in place temporarily with small pieces of sticky tape.

- This box is the perfect size for postcards or standard-sized photographic prints. A smaller box would be ideal for storing a collection of ticket stubs; a larger one might house theater playbills or concert programs.

FABRIC AND
Flowers

Ribbon and Lace

Use "pearl" beads and lace to create an elegant frame that is perfect for an anniversary or wedding photograph. This project uses only a small piece of lace yet shows it off to its best advantage with the addition of the beads. A cluster of wired beads on one corner adds a final flourish. You can make the decoration yourself or use a discarded piece of jewelry, such as an old brooch. In the step-by-step instructions the fabric is stuck to the frame using double-sided tape, but you may prefer to use a fabric adhesive; either way, the glued edges of the fabric can be covered for a neat result, especially if you are making this frame as a gift.

Advanced

You Will Need

- Old newspaper
- Fabric adhesive
- Glue spreader
- Flat frame, 10 x 8 in. (25.5 x 20 cm), with aperture of 7½ x 5½ in. (19 x 14 cm)
- Medium-weight polyester batting, 10 x 8 in. (25.5 x 20 cm)
- Heavy book for weighting
- Solid pink cotton fabric, 13¼ x 11¼ in. (33.5 x 28.5 cm)
- Ivory all-over lace or broderie anglaise fabric, 13¼ x 11¼ in. (33.5 cm x 28.5 cm)
- Double-sided tape
- Scissors

- Sewing thread to match lace
- Sewing needle
- "Pearl" rocailles and flat-disk beads
- 26-in. (66-cm) length "pearl" beading
- Cardboard mat, 8 x 6 in. (20 x 15 cm)
- Self-adhesive paper lace, 27½ in. (70 cm)
- 10 "pearl" teardrop beads
- 10 8-in. (20-cm) lengths of silver jewelry wire
- Pliers
- 2 "pearl" paper leaves
- 18-in. (45.5-cm) ivory ribbon, 1 in. (2.5 cm) wide

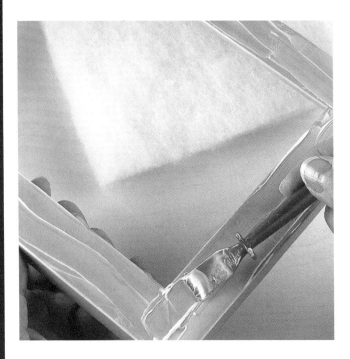

1 Protect your work surface with old newspaper. Using a glue spreader, apply a layer of fabric adhesive over the front of the frame. Place the frame facedown on the batting and weight it with a heavy book. Leave until the adhesive dries.

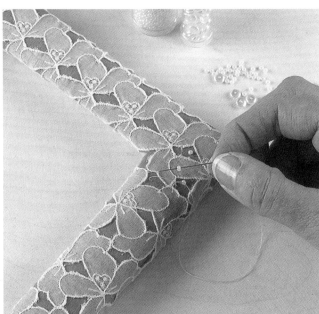

2 Meanwhile, cut an aperture 4 x 2 in. (10 x 5 cm) in the center of both the pink cotton and lace fabrics. Apply strips of double-sided tape to the outer edge of the back of the frame and to the inner edge of the aperture. Place the frame, batting side down, on the cotton fabric.

3 Trim off the four corners of the pink fabric and cut slits in the center, diagonally, as far as the four inner corners of the aperture, then pull the edges of the fabric over the sides of the frame and press down onto the sticky tape. Repeat Step 2, then add the lace fabric. To ensure a neat finish, you may need to stitch the fabric together at the corners. Stitch small beads evenly all over the fabric on the front of the frame.

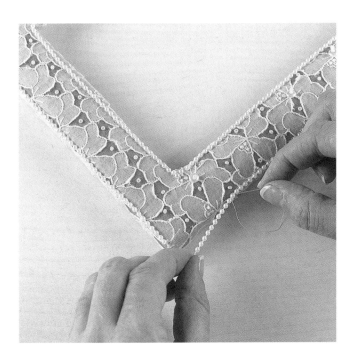

4 Stitch the "pearl" beading to the outer and inner edges of the frame. For a clean finish, cut a piece of cardboard the same size as the frame and stick it onto the back of the frame to hide the edges of the fabric and the tape. Trim the cardboard around the outer and inner edges of the frame.

5 To further enhance the lacy effect, stick a border of lace (in this case, self-adhesive paper lace) to the inner edges of the mat.

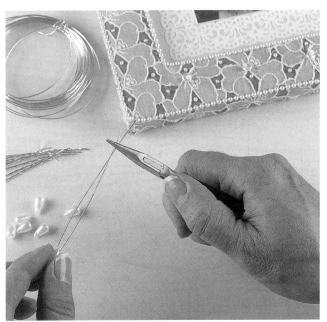

6 To make a decoration for the corner of the frame, slip a "pearl" teardrop bead onto the center of one of the silver jewelry wires. Clamp the two ends of the wire with pliers and, holding the bead, twist to make a firm stem. Repeat with the other nine lengths of wire and beads. Gather the wires to make a small posy, adding the paper "pearl" leaves. Tie the ribbon tightly around the center of the wire stems, then tie into a neat bow. As a finishing touch, stitch a few small beads to the knot of the bow. Trim the ends of the wire stems and glue or stitch the posy in place on the frame. Insert the photograph into the frame.

Forever Flowers

For an elegant look, use a scattering of flower heads to frame a favorite portrait. Real flowers fade, but those made from fabric last forever, like a treasured memory. Easy to make and very effective, this three-dimensional frame features artificial flowers—in this case, wild roses in pretty shades of pink, yellow, and white. When choosing flowers for this project, try to select blooms with flat heads that will adhere successfully to the frame.

Easy

You Will Need

- Frame, 12 x 10 in. (30.5 x 25.5 cm)
- Cardboard mat, 10 x 8 in. (25.5 x 20 cm), with an oval aperture
- Fabric flowers, such as wild roses (see Handy Hint, page 136)
- Scissors
- Old newspaper
- Fabric glue and glue gun
- Cardboard

1 Remove the glass from the frame and make sure the mat fits. Check what portion of the mat is hidden under the recess of the frame so you do not stick any flowers or leaves in this area.

2 Snip off a few leaves and arrange them on the mat; then snip off some flower heads. Try out your arrangement before sticking anything down.

3 Protect your work surface with old newspaper. First stick the leaves in place. Heat the glue gun and apply a thin line of glue along the stem and a small blob on the back of each leaf. Press these in place on the mat. Repeat with the other leaves. Do not worry if a little glue is visible behind the stem, because this will be covered up by the flower heads. Apply blobs of glue to the back of each flower. Try to make sure that the glue covers the area where the flower was cut from the stem, because this will help to ensure that the flower head does not fall apart.

4 Stick your chosen photograph to the back of the mat and place it in the frame. Having removed the glass, you will need to fill up the extra space and ensure a snug fit. To do this, cut a piece of cardboard the same size and thickness of the glass and place it behind the photograph.

HANDY HINT

This treatment suits frames of all shapes and sizes: You just have to choose flowers that will fit. Here, a simple wooden frame measuring 8$\frac{1}{2}$ x 6$\frac{1}{2}$ in. (22 x 17 cm) has been painted the same color as the mat, a pale peachy pink, and then decorated with an assortment of small flower heads.

Memory Box

Here is a great way to preserve your memories: an elegant fabric box full of
photographs with a favorite picture (a clue to the contents within) adorning
the lid. If you like coordinated home accessories, you will like this box;
its fabric cover can match or contrast with other furnishings in the room.
Perhaps more important, it provides a tidy storage solution: a place to file
photographs or other memorabilia. Why not make several to house your
own personal photograph archive? The box used here is the ideal size
for standard 6 x 4-in. (15 x 10-cm) photographic prints. You could,
however, use a box of almost any size. Shoeboxes are ideal,
as long as they are sturdy.

Advanced

You Will Need

- Photograph, 6 x 4 in. (15 x 10 cm)
- Laser or inkjet photo transfer paper
- Steel ruler
- Craft knife
- Scrap white fine-weave cotton fabric, 8 x 6 in. (20 x 15 cm)
- Sturdy box, $8^1/2$ x $6^1/2$ x $4^1/4$ in. (22 x 17 x 11 cm)
- Iron
- 18 x 45-in. (45.5 x 114-cm) printed cotton fabric
- Straight pins
- Sewing machine
- Thread to match fabric
- 24-in. (60-cm) ribbon, $^3/4$ in. (2 cm) wide
- Four $^3/4$-in. (2-cm) buttons
- Fabric adhesive
- Medium-weight polyester batting, $8^1/2$ x $6^1/2$ in. (22 x 17 cm)
- Bulldog clips or paper clips

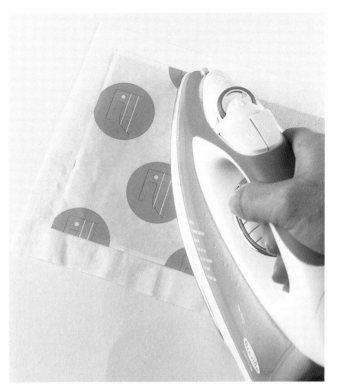

1 Print or photocopy your chosen photograph onto the transfer paper. Follow the manufacturer's instructions and make sure that you print a mirror image of the photograph or the original will be reversed when you transfer it to your fabric. Using a craft knife and a steel ruler, trim the transfer, leaving a thin white margin all around.

2 Place the transfer facedown on a clean, dry laundered piece of white cotton fabric and press with a hot iron for 5 minutes (or according to manufacturer's instructions).

3 Let it cool, then carefully peel away the backing paper. Cut a piece of printed fabric large enough to cover the lid of the box. In this case, the box lid measures $8^{1}/_{2}$ x $6^{1}/_{2}$ in. (22 x 17 cm) and is $1^{1}/_{2}$ in. (4 cm) deep; allowing enough to turn inside the lid, you will need to cut a piece of fabric $11^{3}/_{4}$ x 10 in. (30 x 25.5 cm). Place the printed image faceup in the center of the fabric and pin in place, then machine-stitch all around to secure it. Pin the ribbon in place to hide the join, and either hand- or machine-stitch. Hand-stitch a button at each corner.

4 Spread a thin layer of fabric adhesive over the top surface of the box lid and place the batting on top. Place the prepared fabric facedown on your work surface and place the box lid centrally on top. Clip the corners of the fabric. Smear a thin line of adhesive along the inside rim of the box and stick the edges of the fabric in place. At each corner, fold the fabric neatly, in line with the edges of the lid. Clamp the fabric in place with bulldog clips or paper clips until the glue is dry. When dry, trim off any excess fabric on the inside of the lid.

5 Cut a second piece of fabric, 19 x 16$^{1/2}$ in. (48 x 42 cm), and cover the base of the box in the same way as the lid, omitting the batting. For a neat finish, slipstitch the fabric together at each edge.

HANDY HINT

To make the photo transfer for the lid, you will need a sheet of transfer paper. Various brands are available. Make sure you choose one suitable for the type of printer or photocopier you are using, either inkjet or laser.

Country Charm

For a favorite photograph of a field, farm, cottage, or other countryside haunt, what could be better than a frame covered with a patchwork medley of country-style fabrics? Anyone fond of patchwork or dressmaking will always have plenty of pretty scraps left over, so here is a pretty way of utilizing them. A chunky, flat frame is layered with patches of fabric, some of them enhanced with embroidery. You do not have to be handy with a needle and thread. The fabrics themselves are stuck to the frame with glue, and the only stitching are the very humble blanket stitch and lazy daisy stitch, which are easy to do and don't even have to be neat: Lopsided stitches will simply add to the homespun, unsophisticated effect.

Easy

You Will Need

- Scraps of cotton and gingham fabric in four coordinating prints

- Scissors

- Old newspaper

- Flat wooden frame, $9^1/2$ in. (24 cm) square and $1^1/2$ in. (4 cm) thick, with an aperture of 4 in. (10 cm) square

- Fabric adhesive

- Anchor-stranded embroidery thread in red and green

- Embroidery needle, size 5

1 Cut four pieces of blue gingham fabric $6^1/2$ x 4 in. (17 x 10 cm), four $5^1/2$-in. (14-cm) squares of blue-and-white floral-print fabric, and four $2^1/4$-in. (6-cm) squares each of yellow check and rosebud fabric (or your own choice of coordinating fabrics).

2 Protect your work surface with old newspaper. Apply a thin layer of fabric adhesive to the frame and let set, according to the manufacturer's instructions. Fabric adhesives vary—with some you may need to apply adhesive to both surfaces—but in any case, do not spread the adhesive too thickly or it will soak through the fabric and spoil the end result.

3 On the smaller squares, using two strands of embroidery thread in your needle, stitch blanket stitch (see page 27) around four of the squares and lazy daisy stitch (see page 27) in the center of the other four squares. Smooth the fabric pieces into position, starting with the gingham pieces on all four sides of the frame and the blue-and-white floral-printed cotton squares on the four corners.

4 Once the background fabrics are in place, stick the embroidered squares onto the frame. Insert your chosen photograph.

Sweet Tribute

Flowers are a lovely choice for all kinds of pictures, from single portraits to wedding groups. In this project fabric, flowers, and photograph are all protected under glass, entwined by machine stitching to create a unique and very pretty effect. Choose flowers that you associate with the person or people in the picture, and fabric left over from a dressmaking project or recycled from an old dress. The method used here lends itself to all kinds of combinations and variations.

Intermediate

You Will Need

- Old newspaper
- Cotton fabric, 13 x 10½ in. (33 x 27 cm)
- Fabric adhesive
- Photograph, 8 x 5½ in. (20 x 14 cm)
- Heavy book for weighting
- Net fabric, 13 x 10½ in. (33 cm x 27 cm)
- Sewing machine
- Cotton thread to match cotton fabric and lace
- Scissors
- Fabric flower petals (see Handy Hint on page 146)
- Straight pins
- 30-in. (76-cm) narrow cotton lace trim
- Cardboard mat board, measuring 12 x 9½ in. (30.5 cm x 24 cm), with no aperture
- Wooden frame, 15¼ x 13 in. (39 x 33 cm) to fit 11¾ x 9½-in. (30 x 24-cm) mat

1 Protect your work surface with old newspaper. Place the fabric right side up on the work surface. Spread a thin layer of fabric adhesive over the back of the photograph and place it centrally on the fabric. Place a weight on top, such as a heavy book, for about 10 minutes or until the glue is dry.

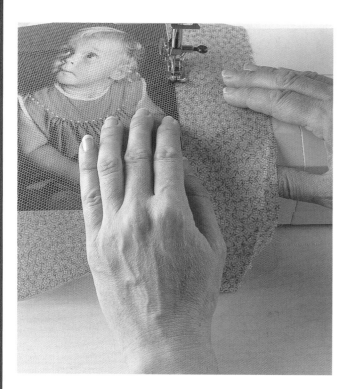

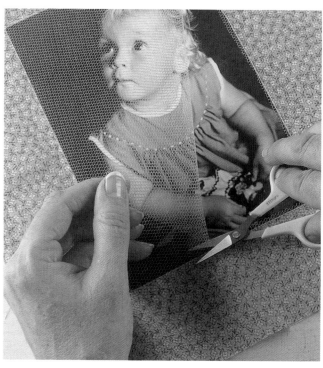

2 Place the net fabric on top and machine-stitch through all three thicknesses, about ¹/₄ in. (0.5 cm) inside the edge of the photograph.

3 Using scissors, trim away the net from the photograph, close to the stitching.

HANDY HINT

The flower petals used here are from fabric flowers that have been deconstructed. In other words, you buy artificial flowers and take them apart. When choosing flowers, select ones that have fairly flat, rather than curled, petals. Some craft shops also sell packs of fabric flower petals.

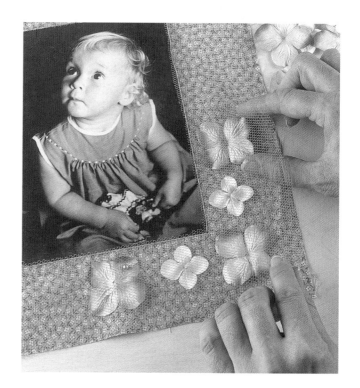

4 Insert flowers between the fabric and the net to form a border around the picture. Hold in place with pins.

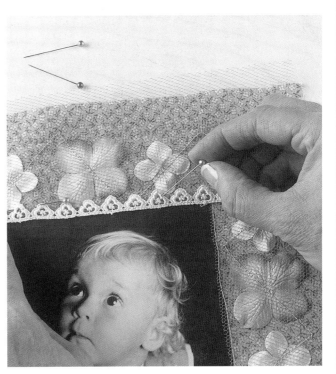

5 Stitch zigzag lines all around the border, making sure the lines go across the center of each flower, to hold them firmly in place; then remove the pins.

6 Pin and stitch a border of narrow lace trim in place all around the edges of the photograph.

7 Place the work upside down on the work surface. Spread a thin layer of fabric adhesive over one side of the mat and place it centrally on the reverse of the work. The fabric should overlap the mat by about $1/2$ in. (1 cm) all around. Place a weight on top for about 10 minutes or until the glue is dry. Trim away excess fabric and place the picture in the frame, behind the glass.

Memory Board

Perfect for a changing display of memorabilia, this memory board is covered with a pretty printed fabric and has crisscross ribbons in which to tuck postcards, letters, photographs, and other items. In this example, a large picture frame has been used, with the glass removed and discarded. You can, however, use a bulletin board as the base for your memory board; simply remove the cork and cover it with fabric.

Intermediate

You Will Need

- Flat wooden picture frame, 17½ x 13½ in. (45 x 35 cm), 1 in. (2.5 cm) wide
- Old newspaper
- Fine sandpaper (optional)
- Medium-sized paintbrush
- White acrylic gesso primer
- Acrylic paint, in red
- Foam board, 15¾ x 11¾ in. (40 x 30 cm)
- Cotton fabric, approximately 18 x 14 in. (45 x 35 cm)
- Scissors
- Heavy-duty sticky tape (such as carpet tape)
- 2¾ yds (2.50 m) pink cotton ribbon ⅜ in. (1 cm) wide
- Awl
- 5 small fabric flowers
- 5 paper brads

1 Remove the glass and backing board, if any, from the frame and keep it for a future project.

2 Protect your work surface with old newspaper. Sand the frame, if necessary, and paint it with a coat of primer and two coats of red acrylic paint. Let dry between each coat.

3 Cut the foam board to the same dimensions as the backing board and glass that you have removed and lay it facedown, in the center, on the reverse side of the fabric. Trim the fabric 1 in. (2.5 cm) from the sides of the board.

4 Trim a little fabric from each corner, fold the corner of the fabric over the corner of the board, and tape in place. Fold the edges of the fabric over neatly, starting with the center of one long edge, and tape in place.

5 Cut lengths of cotton ribbon and position them across the board. Hold the ends in place with sticky tape on the reverse of the board.

6 Where the ribbons intersect on the front, pierce through all layers with an awl.

7 Place a flower at each intersection of ribbon and push a paper brad through, opening it out flat at the back and covering the points with a piece of carpet tape so that they do not scratch the wall when the board is hung.

8 Place the covered board into the frame and tape in place. Insert the photographs as desired by tucking them under the ribbons on the front of the frame.

HANDY HINT

Instead of sticky tape, you may prefer to use a fabric adhesive to stick the fabric in place. Apply a thin layer to the wrong side of the fabric and the board, and place a weight on top while the glue is drying.

Going Glamorous

Generously wrapped and tied with organza, then studded with glistening beads, this rich jewel of a frame would be exactly the thing for a photograph commemorating a glamorous occasion. Organza is a wonderful fabric: Sheer and crisp and shot through with translucent color, it seems to have a life of its own. You can tame it into shimmering pleats and wrap it around a padded picture frame to create glamour and glitz. The frame used here had seen better days. Padded and covered with silk fabric, it was a little dull and uninteresting, crying out for a makeover. You may find a similar frame in a thrift shop or flea market, even around the house. If not, you can simply cover a plain frame with batting and a base fabric, as described on pages 130–133.

Advanced

You Will Need

- 8-in. (20-cm) plum-colored organza, 58 in. (148 cm) wide

- Scissors

- Sewing thread to match organza

- Fine needle

- Padded fabric-covered frame, 6 in. (15 cm) square, with an aperture 2½ in. (7 cm) square

- Small glass lilac and gold beads

- 60-in. (152-cm) pink organza ribbon, ¼ in. (6 mm) wide

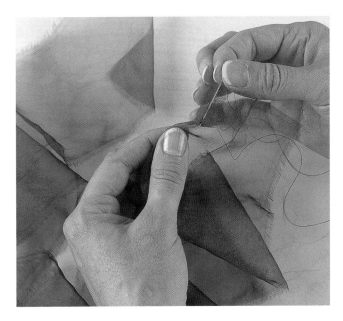

1 Cut the organza in half lengthwise, making two long 4-in. (10-cm)-wide strips. Fold under ½ in. (1 cm) along one long edge of one of the strips and stitch a running stitch through both thicknesses, about ¼ in. (6 mm) from the fold.

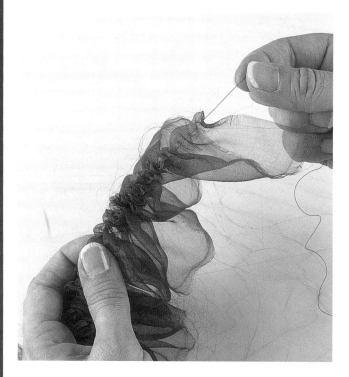

2 Pull up the thread, gathering the fabric until it measures 12 in. (30.5 cm) long. Repeat with the other strip.

3 Each strip will be long enough to cover two sides of the frame. Starting at one corner, slipstitch the folded edge to the back edge of the frame. Continue until you reach the corner diagonally opposite, then join in the end of the second strip.

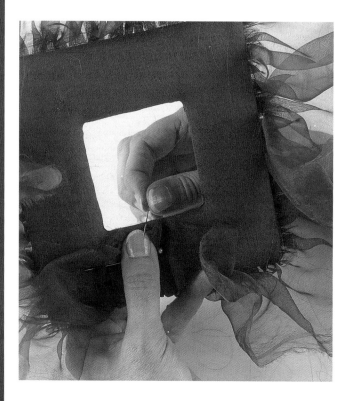

4 Now slipstitch the opposite edge of the strips to the inner edge of the frame, around the central aperture, tucking under the excess fabric as you go and folding under the raw edges at either end of each strip to form diagonal folds at the corners of the frame.

5 On the front of the frame, stitch a border of lilac beads around the aperture and add single lilac beads randomly spaced all over the pleated fabric.

6 Cut two 18-in. (45.5-cm) lengths and two 12-in. (30.5-cm) lengths of ribbon. Place the centers of the two longer strips across two opposite corners at the back of the frame. Hold in place with a few small stitches.

7 Tie the ribbon ends together at the front of the frame. Tie each shorter length around the bows to create two double bows at opposite corners. Stitch on gold beads, singly and in clusters of three, including a few in the centers of the bows. Insert your chosen photograph into the frame.

Wedding Album

This album is custom-made for wedding photographs. Not only can you choose the exact size to suit your own purposes, but you can also select a favorite picture to adorn the cover. Follow the step-by-step instructions exactly to produce an album of the same size and dimensions as the one pictured, which has been designed to accommodate 8½ x 11-in. (21.5 x 28-cm) pages and two standard-sized cover photos, which you can either trim or alter the size to suit yourself; the method is easily adaptable. To further personalize your album, choose your own fabric and trim.

Advanced

You Will Need

- Sturdy cardboard, 13 x 9^1/4 in. (33 x 24 cm)

- Sturdy cardboard, 13 x 9 in. (33 cm x 23 cm)

- Cutting mat

- Steel ruler

- Craft knife

- Carpet tape, 2 in. (5 cm) wide

- 18-in. (45.5-cm) damask fabric

- Pencil

- Scissors

- Old newspaper

- Fabric adhesive

- 2 photographs (see Handy Hint, page 160)

- Glue spreader

- Hand sewing needle and sewing machine and thread to match damask

- 2 pieces medium-weight polyester batting, each 13 x 9^1/4 in. (33 x 24 cm)

- 2 sheets 8^1/2 x 11-in. (21.5 x 28-cm) card stock for inside covers

- Heavy book for weighting

- 54-in. (137-cm) eyelet lace with ribbon

- Hole punch

- 36-in. (91-cm) wired satin ribbon

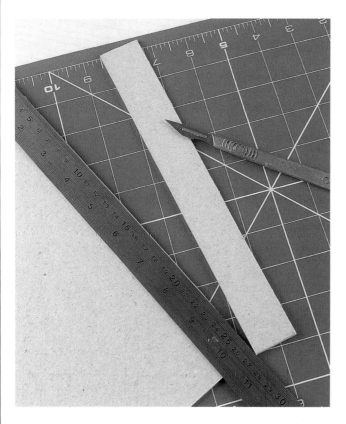

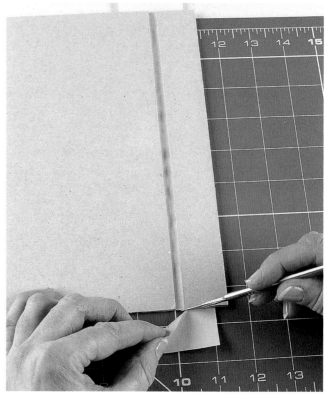

1 On a cutting mat and using the steel ruler and craft knife, cut a 1¹/₄-in. (3-cm)-wide strip off the short end of the smaller of the two pieces of cardboard.

2 Place the two pieces side by side with a ¹/₄-in. (0.5-cm) gap between and lay a length of carpet tape across the join. This will form the hinge on the front cover of the album.

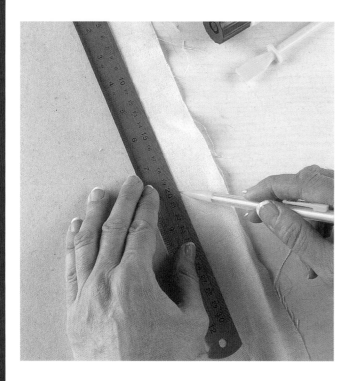

3 Place one of the covers on a double thickness of damask fabric. Using a pencil, draw a line all around, 1¹/₄ in. (3 cm) from the edge of the cardboard, giving you an area of fabric 15¹/₄ x 11¹/₂ in. (39 x 29 cm). Cut out the fabric.

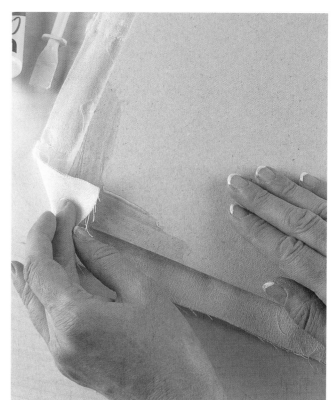

4 Protect your work surface with old newspaper. With a spreader, apply fabric adhesive to the backs of the photographs and position centrally on one of the fabric pieces and cut lengths of eyelet lace to form borders (see picture of the finished project as a guide) and stitch in place by hand or machine, making sure that the stitching penetrates the edges of the photographs.

5 Glue the batting to the front of each cover, then place them, batting side down, on the reverse side of the damask fabric. Use the jointed cover for the front of the album (the one with the photographs and the lace).

6 Glue the edges of the fabric to the inside of the covers. To make a neat result on the corners, hand-stitch with a needle and matching thread.

7 Apply adhesive to the wrong side of the card stock, and stick in place inside the front cover, covering any untidy edges of fabric. Place a heavy book on top and leave until the adhesive is dry. Repeat with the back cover.

8 Mark and punch holes on the left-hand side of the cover and corresponding holes in the pages and the back cover.

9 Thread satin ribbon through the punched holes and tie in a neat bow.

HANDY HINT

Photographic prints have been used for this project, glued and stitched to the fabric cover. If you don't wish to use original prints, have copies made. You could also choose to employ the transfer method described on pages 137–140.

Garland of Love

Wrapped with shiny ribbons and bedecked with flowers for a romantic effect, this frame is perfect for a sentimental photograph, a treasured drawing, or a fragment of a love letter. Search your attic or cupboards for a frame that has been put away because it is not shiny enough to be put on display but too good to throw away. A rusted or tarnished silver or brass frame would be ideal, particularly one with an oval or round shape or with rounded corners. Ribbons come in all colors, widths, and finishes. Choose a color to suit your taste, but make sure it is not too wide or it will form creases—and not too thick, or you may not be able to fit the back of the frame in place. As for the flowers, a well-stocked craft store should offer a wealth of choices; select small blooms that will not overpower a small frame.

Intermediate

You Will Need

- Photo frame, 7½ x 5½ in. (19 x 14 cm) with 5½ x 3½-in. (14 cm x 9-cm) aperture
- 6½ yds. (6 m) of ⅜-in. (1-cm)-wide purple satin ribbon
- Hand-sewing needle and thread to match the ribbon
- Scissors
- 2 yds. (2 m) of ⅜-in. (1-cm)-wide pink sheer ribbon
- 3 pink fabric flowers
- 2 purple fabric flowers

1 Dismantle the frame, reserving the glass and backing for later.

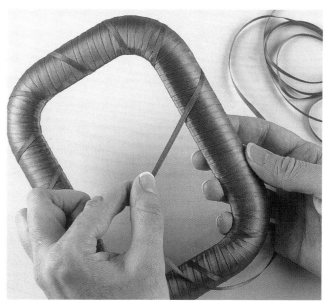

2 Hold one end of the purple ribbon against the back of the frame and stitch the end to secure it in place. Begin winding the ribbon around and around, overlapping the edges to completely cover the frame. Trim off any excess and stitch the ribbon end to secure it.

3 Attach one end of the pink sheer ribbon at the back of the frame with a few stitches and wind it around, this time leaving spaces in between for the purple ribbon to show through. Fasten off the end of the ribbon at the back of the frame with a few stitches.

4 Stitch the flowers in place. Insert your chosen photograph and replace the glass and backing.

HANDY HINT

Stitching provides the neatest finish, especially on a small surface. If you do not wish to stitch the ribbons and flowers in place, however, a hot-melt glue gun is useful for this type of project because it is quick and easy to use and forms a lasting bond.

Templates

PET FRIENDLY (pages 42–44)

NOTES TO REMEMBER (pages 88–92)

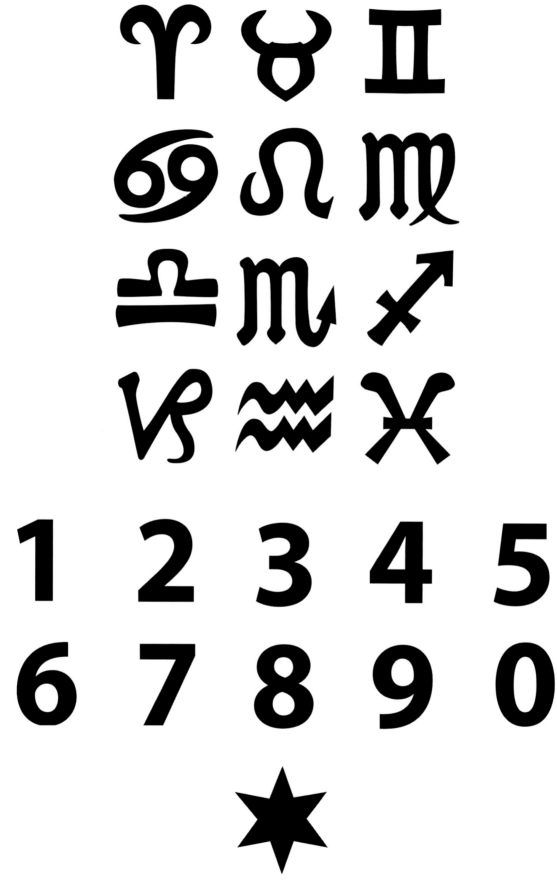

STAMPED STYLES (pages 52–55)

TRINKETS AND TREASURES (pages 56–59)

A GLASS ACT (pages 60–62)

POMP AND CIRCUMSTANCE (pages 72–74)

WARM WELCOME (pages 78–80)

CELEBRATIONS (pages 81–84)

TEMPLATES 171

CANDY AND GLITTER (pages 98–101)

LOVE LETTERS (pages 124–127)

CUSTOM CORNERS (pages 102–105)

Acknowledgements

Thanks to Makit in Cardiff for designing and cutting wooden shapes; to Carol Hook at Clear Communications for providing Pébéo Deco matt paints, gesso and metal foils; to Amy and Andy at Edding UK for Edding paint markers and UHU craft adhesives; to Michael Khoury at Darice Inc. for the wooden memory box frames and wooden heart cutouts; to Fiskars for cutting mats and decorative scissors; to Applicraft for Craquelure, Crackle Glaze and Découpage Finish; to Daler-Rowney for System 3 acrylic paints, gesso, acrylic varnishes, brushes and Craft Seal; to Coats Crafts UK for Anchor embroidery cotton; to Dylon for Image Maker inkjet transfer paper; to Barbara Shepherd at Lakeland for hydrangea petals, metal flower motifs, gem stones and adhesive lace borders; and to Staedtler for Easy Metal from the Eberhard Faber craft range. Thanks also to Rosemary Wilkinson and Corinne Masciocchi at New Holland, to Shona for patiently photographing the projects, to my children Joshua, Lillie and Edith for being such willing photographic subjects over the years, and to my mum and dad for being such creative role models.

Suppliers

Applicraft
www.applicraft.co.uk

Coats Crafts
www.coatscrafts.co.uk

Daler-Rowney Limited
www.daler-rowney.com

Darice Inc., Ohio USA
www.darice.com

Dylon
www.dylon.co.uk

Edding International
www.edding.com

Fiskars
www.fiskars.com

Lakeland Limited
www.lakeland.co.uk

Makit
www.makit.co.uk

Pébéo
www.pebeo.com

Staedtler (UK)
www.staedtler.co.uk